'Having worked with Andy Headington for a numl
a trusted and authoritative source on all aspects c
tells it like it is, offering pragmatic and grounded advice rooted in solid
research and data. His strategic clarity, commercial acumen and ability to
turn complex digital challenges into clear, actionable plans have made Adido
a trusted partner for many in the travel sector, including Simpson Travel.'
Ed Pyke, Managing Director, Simpson Travel

'Andy Headington is a digital visionary and an excellent presenter – his data
driven insights for our markets have been invaluable and have helped to
deliver some impressive results. His presentations to our UK business have
been excellent – as inspiring as they were full of rich content. His distillation
of market trends and clear story on all things AI have been particular highlights.'
Lesley Taylor, Managing Director, Globus Family of Brands

'Whenever I see Andy Headington present his thoughts, or explain his work,
I always learn something new – even after 30-plus years in communications.
Eloquent and engaging, audiences are nearly always transfixed. It's really
worth understanding what he has to say.'
Graeme Buck, Director of Communications, ABTA

'I've known Andy Headington for many years, and his knowledge of digital
marketing is second to none. He has an incredible ability to make complex
digital strategies clear, actionable and effective. His insight, creativity and
genuine passion for helping travel businesses grow have made him one of
the most respected voices in the industry. I've utilized Andy's expertise to
support our company's growth trajectory, and I can see he is someone who
truly cares about delivering lasting results.'
Graham Carter, Co-founder, Unforgettable Travel

Digital Marketing
for Travel Brands

Practical strategies for effective marketing

Andy Headington

KoganPage

First published in Great Britain and the United States in 2026 by Kogan Page Limited

Kogan Page

Kogan Page Ltd, 2nd Floor, 45 Gee Street, London EC1V 3RS, United Kingdom
Kogan Page Inc, 8 W 38th Street, Suite 902, New York, NY 10018, USA
www.koganpage.com

EU Representative (GPSR)

eucomply OÜ, Pärnu mnt 139b -14 11317, Tallinn, Estonia
www.eucompliancepartner.com

Kogan Page books are printed on paper from sustainable forests.

ISBNs

Hardback	978 1 3986 2470 2
Paperback	978 1 3986 2468 9
Ebook	978 1 3986 2469 6

British Library Cataloguing-in-Publication Data
A CIP record for this book is available from the British Library.

Library of Congress Control Number
2025044011

Typeset by Integra Software Services, Pondicherry
Printed and bound by CPI Group (UK) Ltd, Croydon CR0 4YY

CONTENTS

ABOUT THE AUTHOR

Andy Headington is CEO of travel marketing agency Adido. He is a recognized speaker on various aspects of travel and digital marketing, from SEO to PPC, AI and data.

Having spent over two decades involved in hundreds of digital marketing and website projects, he helps to lead a team of 20 marketers, developers and strategists. The Adido team helps travel brands build websites and work on campaigns that deliver more bookings and increase the value of businesses they work with.

Andy is a recognized speaker within the travel industry to has spoken at dozens of leading travel conferences including ABTA, Advantage, TTG, PTS, Uniglobe, SPAA, TTNG, CLIA and many other travel organizations across the UK. He has also been featured in many respected travel publications such as TTG, Travel Weekly, Travolution and Travel Gossip, and has written dozens of research and opinion pieces on the Adido website over several decades.

Andy developed his love for travel from an early age and has travelled around the world to countries like Thailand, Bali, The Gambia, Fiji, Australia and many others. Andy lives in Salisbury, UK and has a keen interest in the outdoors, travel, music and technology.

PREFACE

For some, the word 'digital' has lost its meaning over the years. What was once a well-understood term given to a set of marketing channels eventually got added to almost everything and anything to do with technology and the world we live in. As more time was spent with screens and the internet by all generations, digital has become less of a thing and more of a way of life.

But that's a perspective that perhaps only works for those who have been around the 'digital marketing' world for a long time. For a lot of marketers, the words digital marketing indicate something very unique and defined; search marketing (both paid and organic), social media, email, display and many other channels are all used to reach billions of people each day. While every part of marketing these days has at least some element of digital to it, digital marketing in its simplest form is the use of those channels that can be accessed through a phone, desktop or tablet device. They are 100 per cent digital and for most businesses, including travel, are by far the largest drivers of revenue and traffic. Many travel businesses rely on search, social and other digital channels as their sole way of reaching travellers. Without them, there would be no business.

When the stakes are this high, you'd perhaps expect the knowledge of the digital marketing world to be very high too. However, this isn't always the case. Many companies spend time and money on Google Ads or Meta posts without knowing how well they perform or where commercial success comes from. They have become reliant on channels without properly knowing how they work or how to get the best from them.

Having seen so many good and bad examples in my 20 years of being involved in digital marketing and website projects, I've got a good handle on what's possible, where improvements can often be found and what good looks like. And when I speak with marketing directors or managers to try to offer support to their challenges, I see the same challenges come up again and again. From a lack of knowledge around how Google works, to measuring success and how to get more from social media, the challenges that continue to puzzle and confuse travel businesses day in day out are very similar across the industry.

I have presented to thousands of marketers and enjoyed positive feedback from my talks and blogs I've written. I really wanted to share my thinking with a wider audience to help more people across the globe with their marketing challenges. I have always loathed the rubbish that is shared by so-called experts across the various media channels over the years, it helps no one. I've found in time that my own balanced view of platforms, technology and brands has helped keep a perspective of what actually works and what doesn't. It's very easy to buy into a narrative about a new technology being the best thing ever, and get side-tracked from the things that will make a difference now and in the short term. The marketing industry often doesn't do itself any favours. While the 'next big thing' might take all of the attention of marketers for a while, the main principles of marketing haven't changed too much. But our view of them has been bent out of shape over the years, and I believe that this needs to be addressed.

While this book is all about how to make digital work harder for your travel company, I haven't based it purely on what works now, because the goalposts tend to move fairly quickly, particularly when so few companies hold so much control. Their needs and profit always come first. Keeping to the core marketing principles and long-term ideas will serve you, your bosses and your travellers better in the long run, and I do my best to explain as much as I can through these pages.

While I've written tens of thousands of words over many years for my company and other travel publications, this is the first book I've written. And I did so at a time when the use of AI tools is increasingly commonplace. 'Didn't you just get ChatGPT to write it for you? I would have!' is a comment I've heard many times when I've mentioned writing my book to people.

The idea of outsourcing words in my name and expertise to a machine without any lived experiences, just to save a few hours, goes against a lot of the things I stand for. While I believe that technology is a great enabler, we must use it in the correct way to help us, rather than as a replacement for our own thinking or ideas.

I hope that by reading this book I can not only widen your view of the digital marketing world but also inspire you to make better choices with your marketing efforts going forward. If you have any feedback for me then please do seek me out online and send me a message – I'm always looking to help more people and learn as much as I can from others.

1

How digital has changed travel

Introduction

It's sometimes hard to remember a time before the internet. Having spent most of my life staring at screens and downloading information from across the globe, the idea of a time without the world being connected seems alien, as it must to many billions of people. However, if you've ever tried to get a train across the UK, you'll know that you can still easily get this feeling back without too much fuss.

Dodgy train signals aside, as you read this, right now is the least connected we will ever be technologically. The direction of travel is going only one way. More data, at faster speeds and taking up more of our time.

The idea that the next few decades are going to see a huge row back from where we are to a more modest and offline world is, sadly, to this writer at least, crazy. Digital technology has transformed our world and isn't going away. While many sectors have been quick to embrace change, travel has always felt somewhat slow. Read any travel publication or go to any travel conference and this theme will present itself somewhere along the line. Travel is still playing catch-up and perhaps always will.

Travelling, in all its forms is quite at odds with 'digital'. Travel is about the real world. Discovery. Smells. Sights. Chance encounters. Moments of magic. Digital is about binary. Yes/No. On/Off. The colours of the rainbow that flourish in our senses when we move from one place to another are the complete opposite to technology. And perhaps this is the rub and why so many travel businesses aren't digitally focused. Almost by definition, travel companies are focused on the real world, not the digital one.

But digital is here. It impacts every travel company in the world. From having the most basic profile page on Facebook to spending millions of pounds on ads, and people spread across the globe feeding data centres with clicks, data and sales, *every* travel company must deal with technology somewhere. And every travel company needs to present its best version of itself online. For some, this is in their DNA, the way that they have always done things. For others, it's a huge struggle and one that they still don't quite grasp. No doubt as you read this, you'll know which end of the spectrum you are.

And as you are read through this, my aim is to help you get further away from the 'why aren't we doing things like our competitors' to being the envy of your market. Using digital marketing within your travel company can be transformative.

But it wasn't always like this.

The first travel websites

In the pre-internet era, there weren't many ways to book a holiday or trip. Print media dominated as did the high street. You either had to take a bus or car ride into town, visit a few shops, pick up some brochures and then decide on an option, or you could pick up the phone to chat to someone, perhaps prompted by an advert in your morning newspaper. Any booking made required the help and support of someone else. Even getting a coach ticket required speaking to someone behind a counter and them giving you a piece of paper.

It was just the way of the world and in some ways added to the experience. When I booked my own around-the-world ticket with STA Travel (RIP) in 2002, it was hugely exciting thing to go into a shop with my friends and talk things through before finally agreeing an itinerary and spending my very hard saved pounds. This is still the way that a lot of travel is bought now in some cases, but digital marketing plays a role for the vast majority of travellers now.

Once you were on your travels, navigating the real world required large chunks of paper, too. From plane tickets to traveller's cheques, maps and guidebooks, we had a lot to carry with us and keep safe!

When the internet was first developed back in 1989, no one knew if it was going to be a 'thing'. An idea developed by British scientist Tim Berners-Lee was just that. It wasn't until a few years later that things started to kick into life and other technology companies agreed to work together to bring the protocols designed to life.

Skip forward five years and those who were keen on computers and technology picked up on these developments and started, largely through academia, to create their own 'web pages' using the increasingly common standards set.

By 1995, all types of businesses were dipping their toes into the digital world, with the first purely digital travel publishers like travelweb.com and Viator Systems (still going today!) capturing only a tiny fraction of the travel market at that point.[1] By the late 1990s, a whole raft of new travel businesses were born: lastminute.com to try to capture those with a spontaneous nature (as well as allowing travel businesses to fill up unsold product), Expedia to offer a world of travel options and itineraries, and TripAdvisor to help shine a light on the best, and worst, travel places in the US. These are some that stood the test of time and became global household names. Thousands didn't, for a list of reasons that could fill this book in its entirety.

What these websites all had in common at the time was solving a very real need. Got time to spare this weekend and want to book a trip? Doing so pre-internet would've required reading many different newspapers, making many trips to many shops or calling many phone numbers. New to a city? How do you pick a place to go? Your guidebook could be out of date when you arrive, and you likely won't speak the language, so where on earth do you go and where do you eat? The fear of the unknown has always been strong when travelling so let's use technology to solve it!

The problems we faced then were very different to now. The challenges in 2025 are not about novelty, they are about discovery and, increasingly, trust. We now ask how to better market ourselves online to a potentially global audience rather than how to get connected in the first place.

Early mover advantage

For those people who had the vision in the late 1990s of what the internet would become, it was an incredibly exciting time. Never before had the human race ever been so potentially well connected. What would this mean for existing industries? What would it mean for society? Would it even work out? So many questions were unanswered at that time and despite the great promise of technology and coverage it got, there were still many 'in the know' who didn't believe it to be the future. Many leading publications at the time made predictions that the internet would grow in a bubble of hype and then collapse spectacularly.[2]

These predictions were commonplace for many years. Like today, the media was and is obsessed with the latest technology. Back then it was the internet, today it is artificial intelligence (AI), tomorrow… well, who knows (we'll get to that later)? With any big technological breakthrough, there will always be winners and losers. Those that had the right idea at the right time and made it happen tended to win. Those that were too early or too late tended to attract a lot of hype but then fail quickly.

Even for those that *did* get in there early, it wasn't straightforward. Pressures of money, pressures from the press, pressures of connectivity across cities and countries worldwide made it hard to survive.

When the dot-com crash happened in early 2000, those who predicted a crash and over-investment in the internet were giving themselves a pat on the back for how right they were. 'I told you no one would want to book a holiday online! Look at the crazy valuation of these companies! About time they started to tank!' was no doubt the sentiment from some quarters.

The hype of the dot-com era was very real. The valuations on some companies were absolutely staggering looking back and must have seemed even more unreal at the time.

Take lastminute.com. It was founded in early 1998 and within two years was floated on the London Stock Exchange despite generating less than half a million pounds of profit in the 10 months prior to launch.[3] On the day the company went public, the share price rose by nearly 50 per cent, making the two founders (Brett Hoberman and Martha Lane Fox, who have since gone onto great things) hundreds of millions of dollars in days. But the bubble was very quickly popped and within a month the share price had fallen 50 per cent from its original start or nearly 75 per cent of the peak only a month before. The company was put under all sorts of stresses and strains and for a year or so it was an insanely rocky ride.

For the likes of lastminute.com, Expedia, TripAdvisor and dozens of others who'd already started to establish themselves, it was about hanging in there.

In the early internet era, navigation and discovery of information was hard. Once you found a good website, you would 'favourite' it or 'book-mark it' for later. The internet was also very slow. It was hard to go from one place to another and so it was often easier for users to just click back to one of the better sites that they'd visited in the past and have it load quickly. This first mover advantage for many travel companies was vital.

What made TripAdvisor or Expedia better than the competition that point? Scale. They had more holidays to offer than any new upstart, and this size mattered as it then attracted more people to participate more, and so the upwards spiral started. While competitors have come and gone over the last three decades, the fact that some of these brands were there at the beginning has been one of their core USPs. They have a long-recognized brand and hence still have influence today.

Skipping ahead a few years, despite it missing so many of its targets in its early years of peak expectation, lastminute.com eventually sold in 2005 to travel technology company Sabre for a quite staggering £577 million despite never turning a net profit in the years it had operated. It still had lots of potential as the travel market was still growing at huge speed and it still had a great product (website). But, perhaps even more importantly, it had a recognized brand. At that time, it was one of the most well-known travel brands in the UK, if not the world (largely due to the crazy ride it had been on and the PR coverage it achieved – all PR is good PR they say). Not only that, but the name also started to enter the lexicon all by itself.

'Where's Mike today? Oh, he's getting here lastminute.com.' We all knew what it meant (leaving things to the very last minute). Having that brand recognition in the same way that very few brands ever achieve was and is hugely valuable.

And I could also perhaps look back now and say that the story of lastminute.com perhaps helped to fuel a lot of what was to come. A company with a great idea, but an utterly insane and totally out of this world valuation creating huge amounts of interest and attention from across areas of media, with nothing in the bank to show for it. This approach to 'grow fast and break things' was the mantra of the 2000s and beyond in technology (particularly in Silicon Valley) and helped to fuel the rise of many other technology and travel businesses.

Big winners online

While some of the bigger travel names started to establish themselves post dot-com bubble, there was still massive opportunity for new entrants. As broadband became more of a norm and we started to see the first proper smart phones in the late 2000s, the speed and accessibility travellers had to not only book, but also research, grew exponentially.

As the web became more mature, the cost and ease of which individuals and businesses could set themselves up online came crashing down. What was once the domain of large, expensive and complicated technology set-ups was available for free at almost a touch of a button. Want to set up a website talking about walking holidays in the Cotswolds? Fancy building a range of itineraries of adventure trips to the Cook Islands? It all became more and more of a reality to anyone with a passion for travel and time on their hands.

While technology became cheaper and easier, many travel businesses still couldn't compete on certain areas, mostly around technology expertise and increasingly marketing power. As the internet grew at record breaking speeds in the UK, largely due to a national broadband rollout in the late 2000s, the opportunity grew and grew, not only to offer new travel experiences but to also reach more people than ever. As more people used the internet more often and finding what you wanted became harder, Google became central to our online life.

It goes without saying now that Google is number one, but for quite a few years in the early 2000s, most people didn't use it. Yahoo! would often be peoples home page to get email, news or games. Other internet users had their computers defaulted to AOL.com (when they subscribed to this internet provider), Lycos, Excite or one of many others to start their online journey. As searching the internet became the core feature of our time, we didn't want distraction and noise – simplicity and speed always won out on smaller internet connections. This led to users quickly flocking to Google due to its minimalism and also accuracy which no other search engine could match.

For any business at that time who wanted to reach new customers, Google was the place to go. Their simple to use self-serve platform Google Adwords (latterly renamed Ads) launched in the UK in 2004 and allowed any business to put their name against any search result that was returned for what, at the time, was merely pence per click (a 4p minimum was in place but was peanuts for the value you could get).

As technology reached more people more often, more was possible. But when the financial crash hit in 2008, it put a lot of pressure on people's pockets and so led to declines in many areas of life, particularly travel. Where people once had additional spending power, they no longer did. That solid job of the last decade was sadly gone. It meant that people needed additional income. But how?

AirBedAndBreakfast.com was an idea that started that year as a way for people coming to San Francisco to find a place to stay for the night during busy times where most hotels were either sold out or hugely expensive. Why book a pricey room which you're only going to stay in for maybe 10 hours, when you could stay on someone's inflatable mattress for a fraction of the price?. OK, maybe the inflatable mattress thing wasn't the best idea, but they had to start somewhere, and it worked. The idea of staying in a complete stranger's house might've seemed mildly mad at that point but the service took off quickly with the help of investment and guidance. By 2011, the site had over a million nights booked through it and tens of thousands of listings – many being whole rooms or houses. The rest, as they say, is history.

Last reported revenues of Airbnb.com were in 2024 which topped nearly eleven billion dollars.[4] As well as making the founders billionaires, Airbnb has literally changed the world. Some see it as a full-time job, some fuel their own holidays by letting others holiday in theirs, and some cities see it as a scourge, changing hundreds of years of history.

A simple idea, powered by digital technology and spread by communities of people across the globe within a few years. It solved many core challenges of travel from cost of rooms, to availability and uniqueness, all of which became larger factors as social media and reduced financial spending all came to the fore of modern life.

Digital booking stats and growth

As time has gone on, all areas of travel have become more accessible. From the UK bucket-and-spade holidays of the 1960s and 1970s, to the boom in overseas package trips in the 1980s and 1990s, to the 'build it yourself' travel trips in the 2000s and 2010s, all types of travel have grown thanks to technology. Technology around how a trip is put together and sold, but also around the actual things used to get from A to B. Cars are more readily owned and available than before. There are more planes flying each year. Even bikes and e-scooters are more prevalent thanks to mobile technology. We've probably never had more ways to travel (and at a lower cost) than ever before.

While the options have increased greatly as to where we can go and what we can do, from a marketing perspective the channels available have also grown exponentially, too. In the 1980s, the way that travel was bought in the UK was almost exclusively on the high street – a whopping 90 per cent of travel was booked through high street travel agents.[5] Brands like Lunn Poly and Thomas Cook were on almost every high street and scooped up the vast amount of travel bookings. From a marketing perspective, as long as a brand had coverage in local (and national) newspapers, put some ads in relevant magazines and were in a prime spot on the high street, your job would be largely done. The most amount of promotional work you would do would be to go big and bold in your shop window, perhaps doing some fun activities in your precinct to stop passers-by and some door drops if you had the time and focus. People would've come into a variety of shops, picked up some brochures from a variety of operators and built rapport with staff from a shop over time. With such concentration of potential travellers into such small spaces, it was very competitive and cut-throat.

Aside from travel agents and TV, printed media also played a big role in helping build inspiration. Newspapers were in everyone's letter boxes every morning, with millions of people reading whatever version of the news their tastes preferred. Regardless of the title on the top of the paper, each of them had holiday sections during the week, longer form articles at the weekend (sometimes even in their own separate supplement) and pages and pages of ads from agents trying to promote their offering or destination. On top of that, if you visited anyone who completed any sort of travelling around the world, there would no doubt be various copies of what were to many 'travellers' bibles', namely Lonely Planet and Rough Guides. At its peak in 1999, Lonely Planet was selling 30 million copies per year and by 2007 had 500 different publications.[6]

As the 1980s progressed, the bigger travel agents wanted to continue to grow as well as beat their competitors, and looked to modern technology in the shape of personal computers to help streamline operations. In 1982, large high street agent Thomson Holidays implemented a system called TOP to help them improve the reservation process and help to fuel the growth in package trips that then followed later in the decade.[7] While this was fairly new to the UK, in the US computer systems had been used since the 1960s to book flights. American Airlines created the SABRE system to help manage and sell flights to travellers, and United Airlines followed suit with their own APOLLO system.[8]

While these systems became more prevalent over time, they could only be accessed in the high street shops by travel agents to help find deals for customers or put together trips from a variety of places. The days of making phone calls to various providers backwards and forwards just to build out a trip started to die off as computers took over, sending information in real-time, opening up more markets, types of trips and price points.

The building blocks of connectivity were starting to take shape. So when the internet became a 'thing' in the late 1990s a whole new window over travel was opened to all. We've already talked about how this opened huge opportunities for new types of travel companies to appear through the likes of lastminute.com or eventually Airbnb.com, but what did this mean for travellers? Did more options to book necessarily mean more travellers?

The answer for the UK and other countries was undoubtedly yes. From 1996 to 2016, the number of overseas trips taken by UK residents nearly doubled from around 25 million in 1996 to 45 million in a peak period around 2007 and 2008.[9]

The internet transformed how we book our travel and generated millions of more opportunities for people to book all sorts of trips. In some cases, we went to places more often than ever before. Holidays to Spain, Italy and Portugal have more than doubled since 1996. Long haul countries, thanks to a combination of cheaper cost to travel and huge investment by the 'oil states' to put themselves on the global map like UAE, Qatar and others, have seen increases in holidays in that part of the world in the thousands of per cent.

It's not only the destinations and types of holidays that have changed, but also the way that travellers book has fundamentally changed too. As mentioned, in the 1980s the high street travel agents had about 90 per cent of all travel bookings. Forty years later, this number remained but had almost flipped to online bookings instead. Research is conflicting on the exact number but, according to Euromonitor, 69 per cent of all travel is booked online, totalling $2.7 trillion in 2024.[10] Of the total of 'online' bookings, half of that was made on a mobile device, a technology that wasn't even mainstream until the late 2000s.

FIGURE 1.1 Total number of holidays overseas taken by UK residents pre and post 2008 credit crunch, 1996 to 2016

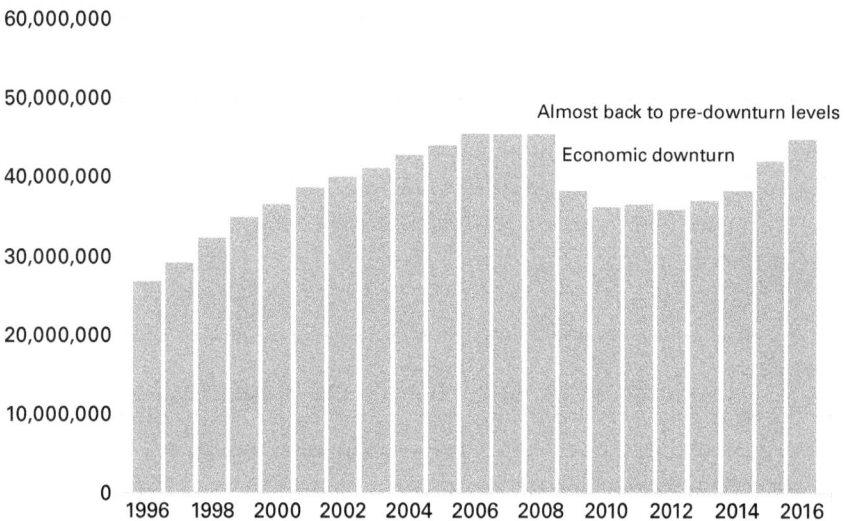

SOURCE Courtesy of Travel Trends: 2016, ONS. Contains public sector information licensed under the Open Government Licence v3.0

It would be easy to predict that the internet will continue to dominate all of travel bookings for the next decade. The booking growth through both mobile and desktop has increased for over twenty years and continues to do so. However, there will be a point where it flatlines. It will be impossible for all travel to be bought through the web. There will always be a market for face-to-face discussion, trust and ease.

And in an age where there are thousands of websites from across the globe offering millions of trips to thousands of places, choice becomes harder. Finding a place to go to, then finding the best options and best prices all take time. Sometimes it feels like a huge amount of admin to do in your spare time and can also suck a lot of the fun out of the process.

Younger generations have grown up in a world where technology has bought everything to their fingertips in near real-time. Want to add up a few numbers? Use a calculator app on your phone. Want to listen to a new song? Load up Spotify or YouTube, search for it and hit play. Want to send a message to the world? Load a messaging app, type your words and off you go. Literally everything can be done in a few touches of a button.

So, when it comes to booking a holiday, where sometimes you have to spend perhaps up to 10 hours researching and planning[11] and nearly 1 in 4 people also say that it's one of life's biggest stressors, it's perhaps not surprising that the younger generation are starting to favour using travel agents more and more to book their trips. If they can pass all that admin to a real travel expert to save them time as well as getting a good price on their trip, then why wouldn't they? Similarly, they are leaning on other tools to help take this stress away, like ChatGPT, which is likely to be used by 20 per cent of 25- to 34-year-olds when booking a trip.[12]

The older age cohort continue to use high street travel agents too. For some it's what they have always done, and a lot of customers have a history going back decades with their agents. Bookings with travel agents in the UK grew by 13 per cent in 2023[13] and indications are that this trend is going to continue to grow steadily, perhaps ending the growth of direct internet bookings.

Inspiration, social media and influencers

We can't talk about the change in travel without talking about social media. Its effect on the globe at large is still only just starting to come clear, but for the travel world it's helped to create a whole new generation of travel entrepreneurs and ways of communicating. For any destination, operator or agent, the idea of not having any sort of social media presence in the 2020s might seem like an alien concept, but it wasn't always like this. Most influencers today are either known by millions or completely unheard of.

Keith Floyd, Judith Chalmers, Michael Palin and Alan Whittaker are perhaps no longer household names, but they influenced nearly every traveller in the UK when I grew up in the 1980s. People would tune in to their TV shows each week in their millions to find out where they were in the world to feel inspired and influenced – a sun-kissed beach, a bustling city or swimming in a lagoon on the other side of the world. These stars and their programmes made travel more appealing and seemingly accessible, and they put new destinations on the map to bring the world of travel into the rooms and minds of millions.

When the internet really started to take off in the early 2000s, we were still largely restricted to terrestrial TV. While Sky and cable were available, they weren't in as many homes are they are today. Accessing ideas and inspiration about new travel locations was still largely limited to TV, Sunday newspaper supplements, magazines and high street shops. Social networking was a thing 'done by kids' at the time as they were spending more time online rather than in front of traditional screens. Media was very slowly moving from something to consume, to something that could be created. The early days of the internet were still limited by connectivity, reliability and speed. But as the decade came to a close, and we saw these issues start to disappear, things started to change.

Social networking, as it was then, had started to run its course slightly. You'd be connected to various work and school friends from a decade before and got to see their new house or where they'd been on holiday that summer, but that was about as much as you really wanted to do. For the social networks of the time, this posed a challenge – how to keep users online and using their platform when appeal was dwindling. Two things started to happen.

The first was that anyone with a decent camera, half-decent internet speed and either the imagination or time (or both) could all of a sudden create their own content. The need for a big production house, big budgets and polished scripts went out of the window. Anyone with a bit of energy and enthusiasm could now start a media channel saying what they wanted and having complete control over their image.

With social networks needing new content for their users, the opportunity to pivot away from a social network to a new kind of 'social media' was one that they had to grasp. More content from more people meant more time online and so ultimately more ad revenues.

The second big change was around how the content was presented to users in their 'feed' (a term that still makes me cringe given it implies we're being fed information like some sort of digital cattle). When content was scarce and connections in the smaller numbers, it was easy to log in a few times a week and keep on top of everything in a chronological order. But with more content being created, the networks needed to come up with the way to show the right content to the right people to keep them coming back.

Enter 'the algorithm' – a piece of computer code that could process millions of new pieces of data each day, categorize it and then use the billions of data points across time and people to decide how to show things to users. Those occasional pictures of your long-lost friend's cat soon disappeared to be replaced with new people you didn't know, sharing interesting content that others had also 'liked' or watched in full.

For businesses wanting to reach more people, and mostly younger audiences at the time, this was another route to market. With millions of people watching videos or reading posts on things relevant to their business, this was a chance for businesses to get in front of huge audiences and for a fraction of the cost of traditional 'old' media. The social networks used the same sort of matching technology to show content to allow businesses to put their adverts in front of the right people too. Has someone been watching videos of trips to Morocco? If you sell Moroccan holidays, you can get in front of these valuable people at a cost decided by the platform. This insertion of highly targeted ads was the next layer of targeting beyond what Google could offer and pushed the value of the likes of Facebook (latterly moved under the parent company Meta) into the billions of dollars within years, with revenues and profit following soon after.

As technology continued to grow and evolve in the 2010s, thanks largely to the acceleration of the iPhone, Android and 4G rollout, which enabled broadband speeds to be reached from nearly anywhere in any city, users became incredibly powerful with what they could achieve for next to no cost. Anyone could become a content creator and start to build out content that would be interesting and intriguing for people just like them.

In travel, a dad of a disabled child could document his observations and hurdles that might come up. A young couple in their 20s might want to travel the world and showcase themselves living their very best lives, but also inspire others like them to take the plunge and visit new and exciting cities. Anyone could write posts, take pictures or film themselves, post it online and start to build out a following. This world of new media, democratized into the hands of billions of people, was all powered by a decreasingly small number of platforms as network effects started to really lock themselves in. Users wouldn't leave as their friends and increasingly 'followers' were on there, and others then saw bigger numbers being achieved by others like them, which then forced them to stay and create more or post slightly more edgy content to get attention... and so on it went.

As the decade went on, more and more of these new media people came to the fore. They weren't just social media publishers; they had influence on others around the world. Their influence was increasingly being seen and felt by businesses in a very tangible way. When a single person in their 20s can get hundreds of thousands of views on a post, with it leading to direct sales for clients, it can't be ignored. These new media stars, now termed 'influencers' for want of a better word, could now command big bucks for seemingly small work.

'Want me to showcase your new cruise line to an audience of under 30s in the US? That'll be $2,000 per post please!'

'Want to get your new hotel in front of your target travellers? Sure thing, just let me stay in your hotel for free for four nights, and I'll do it.'

While the hype around influencers has started to wane in recent years, they are certainly here to stay. Social platforms benefit, the individual (or increasingly their teams) benefits and in the main the destination, location or business benefits too.

A concentration of power

In the Western world, social media has, in the large part, been a monopoly in the last decade. Like Google did with search, so Meta has with social media. Thanks to two incredibly smart acquisitions, perhaps some of the best deals in the history of business, first with Instagram and then WhatsApp, Meta has cemented its place as the global social media platform.

The purchase of Instagram for $1 billion dollars in April 2012 came after it launched its first official app in October 2010. A company that had been operating for less than 500 days (in that form, Instagram was spun out of a previous app called Burbn) selling for $1 billion obviously made headlines around the world. And rightly so.

Inc.com couldn't believe that Instagram was worth $1 billion dollars at the time.[14] They weren't the only ones. With the dot-com bubble still very much in investors' heads from a decade earlier, the money spent on an app which had generated precisely $0.00 in revenue at the time of purchase did seem optimistic.

While the gamble was big, it wasn't based purely on gut feel or hope. It was a very calculated move. With an IPO on the horizon, Facebook needed to make sure that they were not going to become the next MySpace (the equivalent of Facebook, which had crashed and burned just a decade earlier), and any competitive threat needed to be removed sooner rather than later. With Twitter rumoured to be buying Instagram for $525 million in March 2012,[15] Facebook had a choice to make. Go public in a few months with a new tech super group going up against them, adding huge uncertainty in the market, or go big and buy up potentially their next big competitor before they had a chance to get going? The latter was the somewhat expensive, but necessary option. The rest is history. Research from Kantar published in 2024 indicated that by itself Instagram was worth something like $114 billion.[16] The gamble paid off.

In the years that have followed, Facebook went on to acquire messaging service WhatsApp for similar reasons, maintaining the status quo and stopping the competition. WhatsApp was bought for $19 billion in April 2014, only a few years after the Instagram purchase. Again, at the time, spending that much money on a company that had only been making tens of millions in revenue a year, was seen as a crazy move. And even now, a decade later, the company 'only' makes around $1 billion per year in revenue.[17] The purchase of WhatsApp wasn't to really make money. It happened to reach more new users with the Facebook (now Meta) name as well as blocking another potential competitor from branching out into their part of the internet.

Other social media networks have come and gone in the last decade, but for travel businesses Facebook and Instagram have been front and centre of a lot of comms with their audiences. Posting offers, inspirational locations and announcements of new routes is now the norm of business. From something that was for a while seen as the domain of just 'young kids', every travel brand now has a presence of some form or another on at least one Meta platform.

And while I say every travel brand posts onto social media each hour, day or week, sometimes we have to think *why*. When I did business presentations on social media in the early 2010s, it often felt like any brand could get a global reach almost overnight. The speed and scale at which things like the 'ice bucket challenge' (a charity campaign to help raise awareness of motor neuron disease) took off was staggering. From a few friends messing about in a car park to President Obama doing the same thing within a few weeks, the campaign really highlighted the power of a connected world.

This and other 'events' (like the Arab Spring in the early 2010s) put social media on the global agenda and led to more and more people and businesses creating accounts to get involved. As time has gone on it has become the default for nearly all businesses to just post and post and post. It's easy. It's cheap. It's quick. But it has also become incredibly crowded. If every brand is posting regularly, and the algorithms are suppressing organic posts more and more in favour of ads and more engaging content, the chances of cut-through and reach drop each year.

Posting on social media doesn't mean that people will see your content, nor care about it. Travel brands need to really think about what their objectives are and what impact they want to have, before they carry on posting week on week just because others do too. Defining a marketing strategy is hugely important and something we'll get onto later so keeping reading on!

Influencers assemble!

In the talks I did around social media in the early 2010s I would show graphs about Facebook users reaching into the one billion territory. It was a mind-boggling number. Now, as I write this in 2025, we're at three billion users per month on Facebook.

Three billion.

There are something like eight billion humans on planet Earth. And nearly half of them, whether they are in Amble, Amsterdam or The Amazon, are using Facebook once a month at least. I've often predicted that this number couldn't go any higher and there are now some signs that we are reaching a peak, if not a plateau. But I've been wrong many times before and if it reached four billion in the next few years I wouldn't be too surprised.

While Facebook continues to lead the way in terms of active and registered users, there is no doubt that its dominance is coming under some pressure. Again, looking back only a few years, it seemed impossible to think that any platform could come along and eat into its time spent on the platform or get anywhere near as many headlines. While Snapchat had managed to occasionally surface as the next 'Facebook killer' it never made it past a phase of many teenagers/early 20s people's lives before they started going elsewhere. Many other networks were born, had their moment (particularly Clubhouse, which went wild for a month during lockdown when we had little else to do and needed connection) and then popped.

But, just as MySpace ruled supreme for several years in the early 2000s before Facebook took over, there are always going to be trends that come and go. Businesses that rise and fall. And new kids on the block.

In the 2010s, Gary Vaynerchuk turned himself from an unknown online wine seller into one of the most recognizable marketing names globally. His story of determined immigrant business owner, with his New York smooth talking and no frills lingo, mixed with creating content at phenomenal pace and scale, gave him huge reach and a global audience. His ability to talk at speed, with clarity and punch, meant many sat up and listened.

One of his main messages in the earlier days was that businesses needed to stay ahead of the marketing curve, not just be where they are now. Just because direct mail used to work, you shouldn't do it now when we have email marketing. Just because TV ads used to work for big brands, it's a waste of time when streaming is the mainstay of most TV watching and more and more attention is being paid to screens in our hands than the big established networks.

One of the things he did talk a lot about in 2016 was musical.ly, an app that allowed you to lip sync yourself to music and share it with your friends. He talked about this a lot. I didn't get it. Why would any self-respecting man in their 30s want to video themselves lip syncing to the latest Beyoncé track and share it with the world? I get it if I'm 15 and want to do so with my friends, but for businessmen? Or brands? In the UK? Nope. Sorry Gary, you're miles off here.

But it turns out, he was on to something. The app went huge in no time and, as he would repeatedly say, whether it was that app or another that would go big, he was learning new approaches and skills to then use on whatever platform became the biggest, ahead of his competitors. And so it was.

The trend of 'people as brands' had already started and has largely continued ever since. And the skills he leaned into with musical.ly, Vine and YouTube helped to power him to global marketing superstar status, commanding hundreds of thousands of dollars for each talk. And, as it turned out, he wasn't the only one paying attention to the rapid growth of musical.ly. In 2016, the Chinese company Bytedance, had seen success in China with its video-based entertainment app called Douyin. It allowed people to upload and access video content as well as search out people, places and themes.

Within a year of launch it had 100 million users and was scaling rapidly. The owners of Bytedance wanted to go oversees to continue their growth, highlighting that China was only a fifth of the internet and for it to beat off competitors and compete in the long term it needed global scale. And so it created an overseas version of the app in September 2017 called TikTok, an app that used the same tech as it had with Douyin, but with a new look.

With the wind in its sales and big global ambitions, it needed a foothold in more countries and so started buying up other apps with large user bases across the globe. The purchase of musical.ly, still one of the fastest growing and used apps in the US in November 2017, only a few months after TikTok's official launch, gave it an enormous jump with its global plans. Like the other purchases discussed, the price tag of $1 billion in hindsight seems a small sum, but at the time wasn't roundly seen as wise business. An app used almost exclusively by US teenagers (and Gary of course) being taken over by a Chinese tech business could've easily failed but you don't need me to tell you how it worked out.

Video, entertainment and the celebration and promotion of the self are part of the DNA of TikTok. Both musical.ly and Douyin took a short form video approach for self (and edited) expression and found success that was scarcely believable. As more and more time was spent on mobile phones in the 2010s, so we spent more and more time on apps. And TikTok. As of today, TikTok is the most 'watched' app of any 'social media' app out there, commanding roughly 34 hours of time per month per user on average globally, with users using the app a staggering 360 times along the way.[18]

Of all the modern networks around, TikTok has commanded attention like nothing else. The built-in addictiveness of videos being served in full screen, sound on and with hugely relevant content has meant the platform has become highly addictive for many. And this near obsession that users have with it gives great inspiration for people to create their own profiles, sell themselves, and for us travel businesses sell destinations, experiences and trips.

While TikTok isn't for every person or brand, with around 1.6 billion users per month the scale and influence that it has globally is something that we can't ignore for much longer. If you're a travel brand trying to reach an under 35 audience, then it's an essential outpost for you to spread your message. If you're trying to reach an older audience of, say over 55s, then it's up to you how much you want to invest in it (I'd suggest not huge amounts in 2026 or most likely the rest of the decade). We'll talk about channels and choices later. But for now, just know that it is here to stay, and that it commands more attention than anything else.

The title of this section is called 'Influencers assemble' and perhaps this is most fitting for TikTok where more and more people, or influencers, are becoming brands and have huge reach. Some of the biggest TikTok stars have over 100 million followers and aren't 'celebrities' in the traditional sense of having come from TV, film, music or arts. They have built TikTok only followings for, well, just being on TikTok in some cases.

Bella Poarch is consistently in the top ten TikTok rankings for numbers of followers, now into the 100 million plus count. Her videos get millions of plays each time they are released. But her fame started from a simple lip sync video to a popular song of the time. That one video went viral, got a global audience and propelled her into many other areas such as pop music, esports sponsorship and many others commercial opportunities, netting her many millions of dollars along the way.

While Bella and her counterparts aren't going to change how people buy travel anytime soon, there are many thousands of Bella wannabes in the travel world. Where we once had Keith Floyd and Judith Chalmers in the 1990s, in the 2020s we have an increasing number of social media business-people who know the value of building an audience in a specific niche and then monetizing it. There are also thousands of people out there telling you how to do this, which then drives more people to do it... and so on it goes.

What is undeniable, though, is that whatever you or me might think about the merits of a random person on the internet talking about travel or being lucky enough to travel the world while getting paid for it, they are out there. And like Gary V highlighted to us, while things and platforms might change, the basic essential part of humans wanting to watch and trust humans is never going to disappear. We are hard wired to watch other people and still ultimately trust humans over brands or advertising, even if we know that they are being paid to say their messages.

Social media gives the power to literally anyone in the world to create and build relationships with others across the globe. Whether these relationships are anything more than superficial or 'parasocial' (where followers feel that they have a real relationship with the celebrities/media stars they are watching and listening to, even though they don't) is again up for debate. Like them or not, as marketers we have to recognize that they are out there and they can have a big impact on the way we sell and buy travel, who people travel with and where to go.

In the UK and further afield, Dua Lipa is one of the most recognizable pop stars of this decade. She has amassed streams on music platforms going into the billions of plays and has appeared in films, fashion shows and even headlined Glastonbury. She is someone who millions worldwide have grown up with and idolize. And her backstory is one that many have looked into with great depth and wanted to follow. Just as Oasis put Manchester on the map to many in the 1990s or the Beatles put Liverpool on the global radar in the 1960s, Dua Lipa has done the same in the 2020s for her homeland of Albania.

As an Albanian citizen, she has talked about her homeland many times in her Instagram posts, raising awareness of the history of the country but also the issues it has faced. With a following of over 87 million on Instagram and 10 million on TikTok at the time of writing, when she posts, people notice. And some of her posts about her love for her home country have reached millions of people, making it appealing to a whole new audience. In 'peak' 2025, Albania was one of the most booked countries with many travel agents in the UK, with Love Holidays showing a 400 per cent increase.[19] Whether any of this would've been possible or would have happened without her influence is a question we'll never know, but it's safe to assume that the power of influential celebrities is still huge and makes people book certain destinations year on year.

The challenge for Albania and others that are now newly fashionable is how to manage not only their profile in media, but also how to cope with extra tourists without causing an issue not only for locals but also those that do visit. One poor experience from a single traveller can easily spread. Research conducted many decades ago, that has stood the time of time, shows that one person will tell ten people about a bad experience.[20]

However, in the interconnected world we live in, this number can go to millions if things go badly for a brand. In the late 2000s, United Airlines made the unfortunate error of damaging a guitar belonging to a band on tour. The result was a rather miffed guitarist who expressed his frustration on YouTube in a video titled 'United breaks Guitars'.[21] The video picked up over 10 million views and caused lots of embarrassment to the airline as well as undoubtedly losing them many customers along the way. While the days of millions of views for a guitar getting damaged feel a long time ago now, there is no doubt online reputation needs to be managed and monitored to ensure that potential travellers aren't put off.

The fundamental shift to digital

Like every industry, travel has been fundamentally changed by the pervasiveness of the internet in all of our lives. In the 20th century, our media landscape was comparatively narrow. A newspaper a day, a few magazines a month, one or two favourite radio stations and a handful of TV channels. If bad news happened for a brand, then the message could be reasonably controlled to cover up the bad news. 'Spin doctors' were very much en vogue in the

1990s, picking up bad news and 'spinning' it into something low key or even positive for a brand before it had a chance to get into the wider domain.

In the 2020s, the power has shifted away from big media outlets to the social platforms whose algorithms control what gets shown to who and when. Each mobile phone screen is largely personalized to that person and the idea of a brand being 'big' or not can very much depend on the window you look through. One person's Machu Pichu is another's Maida Vale.

Summary

When trying to influence people in this decade and the ones ahead, we need to remember the power of human connection and influence. We need others to show us new things, influence us in new ways and inspire us to take action – both positively and negatively. We also need to remember the world that we now live in. Understanding our audience is crucial to success. Putting together a generic view of who you're selling to, what makes them buy your trips and what they value in a holiday is more important than ever. This is especially true for you in your marketing role.

If you're a 26-year-old social media executive helping to sell overseas tours to over 50s in South America, your lived experience about what is important to you will be very different to the audience that you're hoping to influence. The same applies to, say, an over 40s marketing director hoping to inspire 19-years-olds to take a two-week trip to the Canary Islands. I'd argue that it's perhaps easier that way around as the older person has at least lived some of that experience, albeit in a different epoch; however, staying relevant with 'the kids' is not easy. We'll talk about the importance of audience research and marketing channels later on, but it's safe to say that, to stay relevant in your travel marketing role, you need to keep on top of trends in your audience and regularly check in on them to see how they find inspiration, consume media and choose where they want to go.

Notes

1   C Cossey. History of online travel industry, VroomVroomVroom, 2017. https://blog.vroomvroomvroom.com/2017/05/online-travel-history.html (archived at https://perma.cc/FD57-5QZJ)

2   A Tait. 25 years on, here are the worst ever predictions about the internet, *The New Statesman*, 2016. www.newstatesman.com/science-tech/2016/08/25-years-here-are-worst-ever-predictions-about-internet (archived at https://perma.cc/85V9-LJTB)

3 O Farrelly. Stockwatch, *Guardian*, 2000. www.theguardian.com/business/2000/feb/20/observerbusiness.theobserver15 (archived at https://perma.cc/9XVW-9R2Q)

4 Statista. Revenue of Airbnb from 2017 to 2024, Statista, 2025. www.statista.com/statistics/1193134/airbnb-revenue-worldwide/ (archived at https://perma.cc/775K-9DLU)

5 ATOL. Jet-set through time: Looking back to the 1980s package holiday heyday, ATOL, 2023. www.atol.org/news-and-blogs/2023/07/27/jet-set-through-time-looking-back-to-the-1980s-package-holiday-heyday/ (archived at https://perma.cc/43KQ-XMXC)

6 C Bethea. The 25-year-old at the helm of Lonely Planet, Outside Online, 2014. www.outsideonline.com/adventure-travel/25-year-old-helm-lonely-planet (archived at https://perma.cc/6ENV-BS8M)

7 ATOL. Jet-set through time: Looking back to the 1980s package holiday heyday, ATOL, 2023. www.atol.org/news-and-blogs/2023/07/27/jet-set-through-time-looking-back-to-the-1980s-package-holiday-heyday/ (archived at https://perma.cc/43KQ-XMXC)

8 The Mystery Traveller. How did people book flights before the internet: A retro journey, The Mystery Traveller, 2024. https://themysterytraveler.com/how-did-people-book-flights-before-the-internet-a-retro-journey/ (archived at https://perma.cc/4X6Q-8WNW)

9 ONS. Holidays in the 1990s and now, ONS, 2017. www.ons.gov.uk/peoplepopulationandcommunity/leisureandtourism/articles/holidaysinthe1990sandnow/2017-08-07 (archived at https://perma.cc/Q6PY-HTZZ)

10 Euromonitor. The world market for travel, Euromonitor, 2024. www.euromonitor.com/the-world-market-for-travel/report (archived at https://perma.cc/8SL9-KP32)

11 R Knight. Average person spends 10 hours planning their holiday, survey claims, *Independent*, 2019. www.independent.co.uk/travel/holiday-booking-planning-travel-survey-tourist-a8801211.html (archived at https://perma.cc/4P3U-CWCM)

12 Sainsburys Bank. Holiday planning with AI, Sainsburys Bank, 2024. www.sainsburysbank.co.uk/travel-money/guides/ai-travel-planning (archived at https://perma.cc/TN2R-EG9Y)

13 R Knight. Average person spends 10 hours planning their holiday, survey claims, *Independent*, 2019. www.independent.co.uk/travel/holiday-booking-planning-travel-survey-tourist-a8801211.html (archived at https://perma.cc/NBG2-GD32)

14 E Sherman. There's no way Instagram is worth $1 billion, Inc, 2012. www.inc.com/erik-sherman/facebook-instagram-buy-snapshot-of-a-tech-bubble.html (archived at https://perma.cc/DSW6-GAYH)

15 The Verge. Instagram agreed to sell to Twitter for $525 million before choosing Facebook, says NYT, The Verge, 2012. www.theverge.com/2012/4/13/2946785/facebook-instagram-acquisition (archived at https://perma.cc/DW3Q-EHP3)

16 M Guerrieria. Behind the lens: A snapshot of Instagram's strong brand growth, Kantar, 2024. www.kantar.com/inspiration/agile-market-research/behind-the-lens-a-snapshot-of-instagrams-strong-brand-growth (archived at https://perma.cc/32XC-EYCD)

17 M Iqbal. WhatsApp revenue and usage statistics, Business of Apps, 2025. www.businessofapps.com/data/whatsapp-statistics/ (archived at https://perma.cc/F8QT-CVCX)

18 Meltwater. 2025 global digital report, Meltwater, 2025. www.meltwater.com/en/global-digital-trends (archived at https://perma.cc/UTJ4-S9Q4)

19 Travel Gossip. Loveholidays reveals where clients are booking in 2025, Travel Gossip, 2025. www.travelgossip.co.uk/latestnews/loveholidays-reveals-where-clients-are-booking-in-2025 (archived at https://perma.cc/J82B-LMHQ)

20 Anderson, E W (1998) Customer satisfaction and word of mouth, *Journal of Service Research*, 1(1), 5–17, https://sci-hub.se/10.1177/109467059800100102 (archived at https://perma.cc/R9SA-2VZ2)**21**   Sonsofmaxwell. United breaks guitars, YouTube, 2010. www.youtube.com/watch?v=5YGc4zOqozo (archived at https://perma.cc/ST25-MCXX)

2

Creating a digital marketing strategy for your travel business

Introduction

In Chapter 1 we looked at how travel has changed due to the growth and establishment of the internet. Or maybe it hasn't. Some of the fundamentals of how people buy travel and, well, buy anything, haven't changed and perhaps never truly will.

When it comes to strategic thinking, few have ever got it as right as Jeff Bezos. Like him or loathe him, to go from a starting a digital shop with few hundred thousand dollars, to being one of the top five wealthiest people on the planet a few decades later is impressive, to say the least. His approach to business has certainly worked.

His business strategy is built around the idea of having a laser focus on the things that don't change in the world, rather than those that do. An incredibly simple idea, but one that very few companies follow as effectively as he has. How often have you been tempted to do something (or even done something) to impress your boss or keep up with competitors because 'they're doing it' or just because you thought it might be a good idea without a lot of rationale behind it? I know I have.

Having run a digital agency for over twenty years, there have been times where we've got caught up in the moment or groupthink to invest time and energy in ultimately pointless things. No doubt you will have many of your own stories but here is one for you that will perhaps make you cringe.

In the early 2010s, mobile phones and apps were still quite new to the world. Nintendo were famous for building hardware and games in the 1980s and 1990s and perhaps had lost their relevance and way in the new era of mobile computing. PlayStation and Xbox sales were on the up and up, while Nintendo seemingly hadn't had a popular idea since the Wii, which was starting to seem outdated. When they launched Pokémon Go in

2016, it was an almost instant success, landing it huge coverage and downloads in their millions in weeks.[1]

At the time, some of our team were hugely excited. They would head out for lunch time and then come back to their desks – 'It's nuts out there! Dozens of people are wondering around town looking at their phones and playing Pokémon Go. It's crazy!' They weren't wrong. From launch, it had been an almost overnight success with all age groups. For a week or two the numbers didn't stop and internally the pressure grew for us to do something.

'We have to get on this! I read an article today that said this is going to be the marketing platform of the future. They are predicting that by the end of the year, 100 million people will be spending hours a day on it! Why aren't we getting on this!?' As a recently placed CEO in the company, I wanted to encourage the team with their ideas and create some buzz. But also, having spent the first 10 years of my career in marketing and sales, it didn't really sit right with me that this was our future. Are the clients who we want to target going to be on Pokémon Go? Sure, *some* of them might be. But will they be in a month? Or a year? It didn't sit right with me.

I pushed back with some views on who our target clients were and why it probably wasn't the best use of our time, given that fads come and go. But the pressure from some of the team was building. Do we jump on this craze and be first to 'own' this in Bournemouth so that we increase our knowledge and experience for those wanting to build their own presence in this new digital world? Or do we just sit and let it pass?

Well, dear reader, I buckled.

I let the team play around in the Pokémon Go world for hours to learn more about it and increase our knowledge. We then built out a marketing campaign around being Pokémon Go marketing experts. We built a web page. We got some marketing data and sent letters (yes, letters) to hospitality businesses in the area who we thought would benefit earliest. We posted on social media. We were here to say that we were ready to help businesses in this new and exciting world.

From our campaign, I think we picked up two replies from clients who were mildly curious about what we were saying but it didn't amount to anything more than that. But within a couple of months the people excitedly marching around town and pointing at their phones at random things had largely gone. The hype had gone in the press and the buzz had gone in the office. According to data captured at the time, just three months after launch in September 2016, in the US at least, so had 79 per cent of Pokémon Go's players.[2]

Instinctively it didn't make sense for me to invest time and effort in something that felt like a fad. Our typical ideal client at the time didn't really fit. There didn't feel like there was much longer-term benefit basing a big play around a game rather than a serious or more relevant platform. Ultimately, while we learned a few things by taking action, we made the wrong strategic move. In fact, it wasn't even a strategic move, as we weren't ever set up to be masters of gaming platforms or fast-moving campaigns. It was just an idea that went ahead without any strategic thinking at all!

Ultimately, the reason why we got carried away was because we didn't have a concrete marketing plan and weren't clear enough about what we wanted to do. At that time, we had too many ideas, too many voices and too little direction. While that was a waste, in the long run it taught me a valuable lesson. To make the right decisions going forward you must have a focus on a market and then say no to things that aren't part that. It's part of the reason why I'm writing this book today, as we've spent the last decade becoming travel experts!

My biggest hope for you reading this book is to not make the same mistakes that I've made and many others do, day in and day out – doing things without focus, or because it seems like a good idea without thinking about if it's the *right* thing. We'll look at the consequences of getting things wrong in a later chapter. But how do you build a strategy that is clear and lasts? Let's get to it!

Marketing strategy basics

A marketing strategy is something that every business should have. But my guess is that most don't. Perhaps companies of a certain size do and it's something that gets worked on once a year or periodically as time goes on. However, I think that that those people are in the minority. According to a survey by The Marketing Centre in 2024, approximately two-thirds of small and medium enterprises (SMEs) don't have a marketing plan, and more than half don't have a business plan at all.[3]

Planning is something that most marketers know they should do more of but don't. The reality that I've seen in the last two decades is that nearly no one does. It's sad that marketing operates in an 'as is' way, that things are done 'because my boss thought it was a good idea' or 'that's the way we've always done it'.

I very much hope that, having read this book, you will not be one of those people. Or if you do have a documented plan, that you go back to it, update it, challenge your thinking on some areas and improve it to help your travel business grow.

At the very basic level, your marketing strategy should outline who it is you want to speak to, what your products are, what you want to say, where you're going to say it, how you are going to be memorable or different and ideally what your targets are financially.

Whatever your marketing strategy is, it should align as much as possible to the marketing and sales plan. These two departments should work together to deliver the business objectives, but so many times I've been into travel companies only to find that they have drifted or sometimes work totally separately. Saying that marketing is 'there to generate leads for sales' or other such comments are rarely helpful. Similarly, it can often be the case that sales teams come first – they need more phone calls to keep busy, when digital marketing efforts can only realistically deliver a certain amount at the cost per lead the business can afford. Call centres are often overstaffed due to historical inefficiency. This internal pressure to deliver then often leads to marketing doing the wrong thing, chasing leads for leads' sake and ineffectiveness creeps in.

At the most basic level, your marketing strategy should be minimizing this scenario or ideally preventing it altogether. However, the real world is never perfect. I could count on one hand how many companies I have worked with that had their plans and actions aligned. Often, my team and I would come out of new business meetings and think, 'How is this company achieving so much when so little seems organized?'

Most companies don't have much in the way of plans or alignment and somehow get away with it. But isn't it worth thinking about how much *more* could be achieved by taking a pause, spending time to plan, reviewing the market and then sticking to a game plan rather than throw the most basic things off track by over-investing in something because someone else did it? How you deal with a helpful boss suggesting something like jumping on the latest social media trend because her son recommended it is something that we'll come on to later in the book.

Marketing strategy detail

If you don't know what should be included in a marketing strategy document, let me outline what I think the most important parts are. Each company will do things slightly differently but covering these areas will help get clarity about the most important elements.

- Business details:
  - Who are you?
  - What is the purpose of your business?
  - Business mission and vision?
- Objectives:
  - What are the business objectives for this and the next 3/5 years?
  - What are the marketing objectives?
- Target audience and research:
  - Which part of the travel market(s) are you operating in or want to be seen in?
  - Which customers/travellers are you targeting (and not) and why?
  - What are the demographics and psychographics of your audience?
- Positioning:
  - What are your 4Ps (product, price, place and promotion) defined as?
  - What are your strengths, weaknesses, opportunities and threats (a standard SWOT table)?
  - What are the current trends in your market in the short and long term?
  - How do you communicate?
  - What is your brand tone of voice?
- Channel strategy:
  - What marketing channels are you using and why (and why not)?
  - How do you align these channels? Where do you run your campaigns?
  - What are you expecting to achieve from each channel?
  - What budget is being spent where and why?
  - What tests can you carry out to try to cut budget or grow in new areas (e.g. trying new creative or media)?
- Content strategy:
  - What is important to your audience, and how are you helping them?

○ How can you create content for each part of the 'funnel' (researching a trip vs booking)?

○ What content themes are you going to lean on for ongoing content and bigger campaigns?

○ What assets are needed for each of your channels? How will these get made?

- Budget, resources and planning:

○ What are you spending and where?

○ What are you going to measure – website visits, followers, sign-ups, leads, calls, revenue and everything else (on a spreadsheet by month)?

○ What team members do you have and what will they be responsible for?

○ What needs to be achieved by when (a plan across the year would be helpful here!)?

I truly believe that certain areas in this list are more important than others. I feel it's important to explore some of them in more detail below.

Market and audience research

Of all the areas that a marketing strategy should contain, market and audience research is one of the most fundamental things about it and is so often overlooked.

'Market research? Why do we need to do that? We've been operating for 22 years already! We know who we sell to and why! We can't afford to spend anything on that – we need to pay our Google invoices and get more clicks!'

Ok, this isn't exactly verbatim but it is the type of conversation that I've had too many times. I would argue that 10–15 years ago a lot of travel businesses might've got away with this type of mindset. Google was not quite as monopolistic as it is now. The pay-per-click (PPC) auction wasn't quite so competitive. Search engine optimization (SEO) tactics were basic and getting good results was more easily achievable. Getting good quality clicks was easy to come by. When bringing traffic to a website is seemingly easy, low cost and profitable, why bother with a marketing strategy or, heaven forbid, market research? We know we can get clicks and sales from the internet, why try harder?

Digital marketing has undergone some macro changes in the last 10 years and will do so again in the coming decade. We'll look more at that later. But at this point in our digital lives, Google is not our friend (and hasn't been for quite a long time), social media takes up hours of our lives each day, and tracking is harder than ever. This broad mix means that the days of quick, cheap and easy are long gone.

Marketing is now more complex and complicated than ever, and we need to spend more time thinking and planning to make the right decisions. It's not quite a game of monopoly yet, but we're moving from a game of chequers to a game of chess. We need to ask more questions of who we are trying to get recognition from and persuade with our marketing, rather than just buy clicks from digital platforms. Standing out and being memorable has always been a challenge but it gets harder each year.

Understanding as much as we can about who we're talking to, what is important to them and how we can help them with their travel needs is crucial in order to try to make better choices and win more often.

How to start: Audience profiling

Let's say you wanted to start a new travel company today – who would you want to target and why? What holidays and trips could you sell? And to whom?

You can look at this is several ways. Do you start with the products that you might already have some knowledge about and are happy to sell? Or do you look at the audience first and then find out what opportunities there are to sell to them? Both approaches are valid, you have to start somewhere!

If you've spent most of your previous time in travel selling luxury yacht trips, you might not be cut out for selling short haul holidays to Europe. If you understand the luxury customer, then it makes sense to find out more about them and what their lives are like, to then form some better ideas about new types of travel to sell.

Whatever way around you do it, you need to write down what your target audience is. And it's important here to be as specific as possible about it. The more definition you can build about specifically who you are selling to, the better. Creating an ideal customer profile (ICP), customer persona or pen portrait, or whatever you want to call it (the name tends to change every five or so years from my experience!), will help you to get better clarity about who these people are, what is important in their lives and how best to reach them. It gives you and anyone else you work with clarity about the decisions you then make.

If you're targeting families who want to take a week's holiday aboard together, it is highly likely they will include a parent or parents taking the children. So that could be perhaps anything from three to maybe six people. Would you want to target larger family groups? If they are families with children, you could assume the bookers of the group are aged from 25 to 55. Within that range there any several age generations – do you lean more into 1970s or 1980s references or those from the 2010s? Being generic across the language you use in your content could mean you end up appealing to no one. You have to make a choice. Do you want to target fairly affluent areas like major cities or more specific areas like the southeast of England? What about overseas travellers too?

With digital marketing and the major platforms that can be used, our ability to get specific about who we want to reach and with what message is incredibly powerful. There are many layers of settings that can be used to narrow down who, when and how we want to get in front of people. This can also be overlaid with our website and customer relationship management (CRM) data further down the line to feed the platforms better data about what success looks like and how to then make further improvements. As a data person, this the exciting part (although far too often frustratingly hard!) so we'll talk more in depth about that later.

The one big part that I think is often missed when building personas or ICPs is to also be explicit about who you *do not* want to target. While it's good to be positive and outline our best types of travellers, I have often found it useful to think about those that are either far removed from the ones we don't want to target, or, more helpfully, those that are perhaps on the periphery.

Going back to the example above with our new villa company, do we want to just look at single families with up to six guests or do we want to include larger groups as part as our offering? There is a very valid reason to say that we want to target both, right? Some years our families might travel by themselves, but in other years they may bring parents or sibling and their families too. This could take our villa range from three-bedroom properties to double that or more. If we broaden our range, it could mean more properties to manage, increased complexity when it comes to sourcing and listing, and having to go even wider with our messaging and targeting. There is nothing wrong with that, but it can bring in a weakening of our position of just serving families. It needs to be thought about in terms of a 'negative persona' to make it clear internally that we *only* deal with small family groups.

Building out your ICPs can be done in many ways. It can come from your own head if you have experience in a market from previous roles and jobs. It can come from your internal team, where, rather than you coming up with all of the ideas, it can be from a group session where you might get together people from product and sales teams to get them to answer some of the questions outlined above. A typical workshop might then involve lots of sticky notes being put onto the walls of your meeting room to see what your team think about what to sell and to who. Or, if you are a larger company, you can pay for data from third party company who exist to provide this information from dozens of data sources. They have done all the legwork to provide extensive details about exactly who the people you want to target are and how to get to them.

On top of this, there are many travel publishers that carry out regular research on current travel trends and buyer information that are worth keeping an eye on. In the UK, ABTA do an annual travel trends piece of research that looks at many key data points about how people research and buy trips, what influences their decisions and where they want to go. Signing up to newsletters from travel publishers is another way to keep on top of market trends to help shape and reshape your target audience.

Whatever approach you take to build out your audience profiles, you need to do this as one of the first parts of your digital marketing planning. Once this has been agreed upon, it should then help to lead your marketing plans from website design to ad creative and asset choices, and any other activities that you do.

Audience research

Once you've built out the ideal customers on paper, it's then worth seeing what they get up to in real life and iterating your initial ideas about how to speak to them. You need to validate your ideas with real people. There is always going to be some backwards-and-forwards discussion here to update and revisit your ideas. Do you start with the interviews first, or draw on your own experience and then revalidate and adjust? Most likely your travel business has been operating for many years so you already 'know' your travellers well; your research should back up your initial ideas and change them, rather than completely alter your approach.

Whichever way you do it, speaking to real people and observing them is one of the biggest things that can help to improve your planning. In a world where nearly everything is done through a mobile phone or desktop screen, getting out and about to speak to real travellers about their best and worst parts of the holiday journey is worth so much. The insights that you can get from a handful of chats to your current or future travellers should open up so many doors in terms of what you could and should do next.

It's been said that speaking to just five people can help you uncover 80 per cent of the issues on your website when it comes to finding improvements.[4] While this is true for your website specifically, doing it for product or customer research doesn't need a lot more. Some researchers believe that you can conduct a test with five reviews but find it more effective to continue testing until you reach a saturation point of gathering no more new information.[5] Others suggest a number often between 10 to 30 participants.[6]

Speaking to five clients or more about a range of topics should be your minimum, but is essential. It will help reshape many of your ideas and biases to improve your overall thinking.

The questions you ask your customers need to be very well thought out before just diving in. There is a certain art to building out customer research questions and writing them in a way that is clear, concise and with any bias minimized.

Some helpful tips are:

- Write your questions in as neutral language as possible so you don't lead someone into an answer.

- Provide real clarity about what you want someone to do, rather than just assuming they will know what to write or share.

- Write your questions down, go away from the screen for an hour or a day, then come back and re-read them for any possible misinterpretations or ambiguity.

- Ask someone to read through them and make suggestions (this could be a colleague, a friend or even an AI assistant).

- If asking some to score something to get an opinion, offer an even number of answers to push people to going one way or another (e.g. a score from 1–6).

- Qualitative measures are just as important and quantitative ones! Have a good mix of both to garner opinion on subjects (e.g. asking a question to rate the overall trip from 1–10, then asking why they gave that score, to get some more context).

- When speaking to people, take note of anything that comes up in conversation that doesn't necessarily fit into your questions. Some people love to chat and will tell you lots of additional things that you didn't originally plan for – be ready!
- Finally, try to sense mood and feeling when people are talking. Are they happy, stressed or annoyed when they talk about certain things? These hidden 'clues' can again help to reshape some of our thoughts about what really matters, sometimes more than any actual data captured can.

The real value of audience research carried out this way is that you get to pick up on all of the messy and often contradictory human things that make us who we are. While we can collect our research by sending it out via email or social media, by just collecting the data, we only collect a part of the story.

The unfortunate thing about research though is that what people say and what they do is rarely the same. While we have very good intentions to behave in one way, often the reality is quite different. This has been highlighted many times throughout decades of marketing thinking, perhaps most notably by David Ogilvy, and is often referred to as the 'say–do' gap these days.[7]

This isn't to say that audience research is useless. Far from it. It's just that we have to be careful about how much we rely on it as our sole tool. It should be used to inform our thinking rather than completely dictate it. If we always did everything our customers wanted, we'd never have the iPhone or many other things that have changed our lives.

A theme that I will come back to throughout this book is that digital is great at many things and gives us so much opportunity. But we shouldn't always default to it to get our jobs done, or think that digital is the best way, just because it is often the easiest or quickest. As my career has developed, one of the biggest things that I've learned is that human-to-human contact where we can use our senses and be with each other, even through a screen, gives us so much more insight and data than just raw data does.

'Spreadsheet culture' is everywhere in digital marketing and while it serves us a great purpose, it shouldn't be the only thing we do or use to help us in our marketing jobs. Sometimes the greatest insights and ideas can come from tiny snippets of conversations that you just can't capture through online form filling.

As well as speaking to customers face to face, online customer research should also be part of your process. Having additional data being collected from your email marketing subscribers or social media followers should of course be part of your overall view. But it's very easy for that data to be poor quality if people are only incentivized to do so for a voucher or something else on offer. It's also very common to get low percentage numbers of form fills. Everyone has so much digital admin to do that helping a company that they probably don't know very well for little gain isn't very high on many peoples lists!

Having a mix of online surveys and real-world data collected manually from people is great, and getting between 10–30 respondents is ideal. Research data from digital sources where you believe that audience to be aligned with your target is a great supplement to this. You must be careful online that the audience you collect data from truly reflects your target travellers. It's very easy to get data online which isn't accurate and it can potentially give biased answers which will send you down the wrong path. If you are able to get quality data from both online and offline it is the best outcome you can end up with to help create genuinely helpful customer research.

Putting research into action: An example

Let's look at how some travel companies put their customer profiles together shall we? Table 2.1 and the following box illustrate one example from a recent travel client who, like our example earlier, sells villa holidays in Europe.

TABLE 2.1 Customer profiles

	Zara (Multigenerational family)	Faye ('Friends with kids')	Sophia (Out-of-season preschool)
Goals	Laid back location, freedom, something enjoyable for everyone.	Creating memories and experiences with family and friends, lots of fun for all.	Premium holiday that allows for private time together as a family.
Motivation	A well-deserved break for hard-working husband, memories for children and grandparents.	Wants a holiday that appeals to her as well as the children. Wants to prove children don't limit holiday choices.	Reconnecting as a family, re-setting from a busy city life.

(continued)

TABLE 2.1 (Continued)

	Zara (Multigenerational family)	Faye ('Friends with kids')	Sophia (Out-of-season preschool)
Frustration	Finding somewhere that everyone would enjoy. Choice overwhelm.	Finding a lot of package and conventional options – wants something different.	Finding a good location that also offers everything the children need. Lack of convenience in booking process.
Additional	First time booking a villa holiday with kids so unsure what to plan for. Looking forward to spending time with her husband while her parents babysit.	Needs to find the balance – holiday needs to be safe for children with the opportunity to explore.	Very firm idea on what she wants and expects.

ZARA'S CUSTOMER PROFILE

Zara is a social butterfly, focused on juggling work, family life, friends and fitness (gin and tonic is essential to take the edge off).

She lives in St Albans, but isn't a posh yummy mummy. The family is comfortable, but both Zara and her husband Alex work hard to maintain their joint income and think wisely about purchase decisions. They have two children (Ben, 8 and Lily, 5) and a dog.

Zara works part-time in a job she loves in interior design. She's not fussed about being picture perfect on Instagram, and instead uses social media to stay up to date with friends and family. She's a busy person in all aspects, and often neglects time for self-care. If her family's happy, she's happy.

Booking a holiday can be overwhelming for Zara as she wants to get it right and please everyone.

Her favourite brands are Zara, Oliver Bonas and ASOS. She could afford Tesco but shops at Aldi because she isn't proud. She gets inspiration from Pinterest, social parenting sites like Mumsnet, and her mum friends.

Desires: A holiday that is a special treat for everyone: hard-working husband, mum juggling everything, two kids and the grandparents.

Challenges: Zara is responsible for booking the holiday, but they've not stayed in a villa as a family before. She's a bit stressed, not sure what to expect, feels overwhelmed at the level of choice and wants everything to be perfect, as well as safe.

This is the type of thing we see from time to time with our clients, although often we're not provided with things like this as they don't exist! Don't be one of those travel businesses please!

How 'good' is this as an example? It is a helpful tool as it breaks down the three identified types of potential buyers that they could target alongside a breakdown about who they are, where they live and what their life circumstances are.

In this instance the client has outlined some good detail about each target person, although perhaps not gone far enough about their media diet, how long they spend online, the places that they hang out, what influences them and what they don't like. We have a nice outline of their lifestyle, but I would take this further and make explicit the things that we do and do not want to show to Zara, or the things that make her happy or dissatisfied. I would clearly outline the messages that she is likely to respond to, the phrases that she might type in at various stages of the research process (for our content and PPC campaigns) and what imagery might best suit her (for email, social and website). The more depth and detail we can add, the better and clearer our planning will be.

Far too often, once this part of our customer and audience research is created, and we feel happy that we've ticked a box off, we leave it in an online folder or inbox and don't look at it again.

MAKE THEM VISIBLE!

Print a picture of your personas off and put them around your office (home and company) so that they can remind you of who you're targeting and you don't forget about them.

Positioning and the 4Ps

Many of the people working in travel marketing find their way to a marketing role through various routes, not just via education. Often, someone working on a product team, or in sales or operations who shows an understanding of one or two platforms is then given a new opportunity to learn and fill a role in the business.

When it comes to thinking about marketing and planning, the 4Ps are some of the most important aspects to think about. First developed by Neil Borden, a professor at Harvard University in the 1950s,[8] they have become a guiding light for millions of marketers since. The 4Ps help us to think simply about the main factors of what we sell and how to help us get clarity about what levers we can pull to help push things forward.

Detailed definitions of the 4Ps will always vary depending on who you read but here is my take on them.

Product

Very simply – what are you selling? Are you selling luxury, tailor-made trips to the Maldives for high net worth couples, or one-week fly-and-flop trips to Italy? Are you specialists in one country or a travel agent offering a wide range of options to everyone? This might seem obvious. But often, when it comes to a marketing strategy, many companies won't have this written down. If you asked five people in your business you might get five different answers, and sometimes this lack of clarity causes issues.

Having worked with dozens of travel brands, I have seen many times that travel companies' product lists become weakened over time. 'As an Asia holiday specialist, why are you also selling trips to Croatia and Belgium?' 'Ahh, well, there is a story behind that...' or 'To be honest I don't know!' are things we see too often. What started as a 'simple' travel business product line gets added to, blurred and bastardized into something more complex and different.

I want you to read this book and look at everything that is happening in your travel business. I want you to take a step back and review what you are selling and ask, 'Is this right for us for the next three years?' If you are doing what I have described above, then you have to ask, why do you want to sell to Belgium and also Japan? What does that do in the customers' eyes? Can you really say you are an Asia expert while selling trips to mainland Europe?

I'd think it would cause a lot of confusion and mistrust among customers who are interested in either of these destinations and harm your chances of success.

Making your product choices simple and clear to understand will make it easier for your customers to trust in and stay loyal to you.

As well as thinking about your human customers, for most travel businesses Google is one of the biggest customers you have to cater to. With Google accounting for anything from 20–80 per cent of most travel websites traffic, you have to be very mindful of what they want and then what your customers will see when your website loads. If you want to list out some of your locations and trips by type, how much are showing in each area? Lots of times, we've had clients run campaigns across PPC or SEO or social as they want to cover as many locations as possible.

However, from a potential customer perspective, if I want to find a food tour in Morocco and click on your website that has only one or two listings on it, is that really going to convince me that you've got the best option for me to spend my money on? While we want to keep things simple, one of the hard things about travel is that buyers usually need to see lots of options to convince themselves that they've done enough research to pick the best trip. A website listing with just a handful of choices (or sadly even sometimes no results) is just a waste of time and budget. Having the right locations, and enough variety and quantity within them, is really important when it comes to making the most of your product listings.

Price

How much are you charging for your product? It's pretty simple, right? In some ways it can be, but in other ways it can be incredibly complex. Particularly when it comes to most travel companies. A touring holiday around the vineyards of Southern France could perhaps encompass:

- flights
- coach/transfers
- multiple restaurants
- multiple hotels
- multiple vineyards
- tour managers

There are so many variables that go into making packages, and each of the elements comes at a price. An increase in fuel costs at a macro level would affect every part of your supply chain and cause one of two things – either you put your price up to your travellers or you take a hit on your own profit margin.

Compare this pricing model to a digital marketing agency; the main variable there is staff salary, some minor expenses, and that's largely it! The elements that go into pricing a 'product' are far simpler than organizing a travel product (although, please don't let that fool you, many agencies make next to no money, but that's for many other reasons like lack of process, competition from both freelancers and big agencies cutting prices, and various degrees of client and practitioner knowledge).

As a result, many of the clients we speak to are very vague about how much money they make per trip. Taking our vineyard tour example above, how much you make per tour will vary greatly depending on how many passengers you book onto each tour. Do you have 10 or 20 booked for the tour? The profit per person and trip is going to be very different depending on how many people book your product.

Regardless of actual numbers, there should be a figure available to work out how much each trip costs as a minimum level of people attending, and what that profit looks like, as well knowing what the profit margin will be on top. For example, if the break-even cost of running a trip for 10 people is £1,983.47 per person, then you need to think about how much profit your business is aiming for on top of this. A simple 10 per cent profit margin would mean a final selling price of £2,181.82. How you then present this is up to you. I'm not a fan of showing pence in the price but that's your personal choice. It's also worth noting that a simple 10 per cent margin doesn't account for business taxes, such as Corporation Tax in the UK, which also needs to be factored in at the relevant rates, and will likely push the cost up further.

While it's very important to know what your break-even cost is and what your target profit margin is, this isn't the only factor that you need to consider when it comes to pricing. No travel business operates in isolation and no traveller buys from one place. Modern society is driven by capitalism. The market is there for many companies to offer their products at whatever price they want. And that may mean they offer the same product as you at a lower price. Or vice versa. The components that go into a lot of travel businesses are often unique, so comparing one against another, even though we have more information than ever at our fingertips, is very hard.

Whatever price you're coming up with does need some context in the customers' eyes. Are your prices fair? Are you 'expensive'? Or too 'cheap'? It's crucial to know where you sit in the market and be happy with this position. Apple sell mobile phones. Samsung sell mobile phones too. I don't need to tell you which has the higher price and makes the most profit.

Apple made a choice about pricing despite the fact that on a rational like-for-like basis, their phones are 'expensive'. But it doesn't stop them selling them in their *hundreds* of millions each year and they have managed to do so for more than a decade.

While travel is perhaps more of a price sensitive purchase, it is one that is perhaps under thought about when it comes getting your pricing right. Half of travellers say that getting the 'best price on travel' is important to them when buying a trip, and it is often the number one consideration for travellers.[9]

But travel is a very emotional purchase. The feeling of walking through a jungle in extreme heat, or sampling new smells in a market, or that blast of heat when you step off the plane in a new country… these are human feelings that are hard to put into words but can be pulled on when it comes to justifying a small increase in your pricing.

PRICING REALLY MATTERS

I have worked on many travel marketing campaigns over the years and in my experience it's so important to consider price as part of your marketing strategy. One of my biggest gripes about the role that digital marketing plays is that it is an 'add on' to the overall marketing strategy. By the time the marketing plans are put into action (if it at all), the price of the product has already been decided. A head of product/operations/commercial/sales has worked really hard with the suppliers, internal teams and the board to come up with the 'right price' for each tour, villa, trip or whatever you are selling.

In my experience, it's then up to the digital marketing person or team or agency to then make leads and sales happen as if everything is already definite and it's a simple job of making Google 'work' to then generate bookings and profit.

But customers are not silly. They take time to research, review and plan. An impulsive weekend away isn't booked from one website visit. Even if you offer something that isn't available anywhere else, travellers will have to weigh up what you offer, what you charge and how trustworthy you are against someone else. But if you do offer something very similar to another operator, then price will be directly comparable. No matter how good your campaign is in terms of set-up, creative, website and booking experience, you will struggle to get bookings.

One client sells one villa at one price, while another sells the same villa on their website for the same week with the same options and features for 10 per cent more. Unless that first company has a particularly poor website experience (and/or poor third-party reviews) the second company doesn't stand much chance of success.

For digital marketing to truly succeed for a travel business, there must be a real and proper conversation between the marketers and the product team. Digital marketers (that's you!) need to do the research against your main competitors on both search and social platforms to ensure that your price is in line with what your customers are expecting. If you're higher or lower than the average you need to be comfortable with this from a strategic view and ensure that everything around your brand promotes that in the right way. There are many points that I want you to take away from reading this book, but this is one of the most important.

So much effort, time and money is wasted by having a disconnect between your pricing and your promotion. It is one of the biggest gaps I see in how digital marketing campaigns run and one that you may need to push back on to help your business improve overall performance. I'll cover *how* to do that later in the book. For now, just make a mental note that this is incredibly important.

Place

Where you decide to sell and market your trips and tours is also crucially important, too. I would say that's one of the main reasons for this book even existing! With so much time, energy and money being put into digital media in the 21st century, it's no wonder we all want to know how to master it and generate more bookings.

Historically, when marketers have referred to place, it's usually been for a wider remit than digital, which didn't properly exist until the 1990s. So in those days, where you put your message, the media you used and how you stood out were probably thought about more.

For most travel brands up to a certain size, digital media is probably one of the only places that they invest their time and money. Google Ads are still one of the biggest chunks of media spending that happen across most of the travel world (for some clients up to 80 per cent of all of their website traffic – eek!), with other channels like organic search and email also appearing regularly.

Social media is also a huge driver of marketing activity, with most travel businesses posting onto many different accounts, sometimes many times a day. However, in terms of driving direct traffic to websites, more often than not social media postings do not generate much compared to other channels. Research from SparkToro carried out in 2024 showed that the biggest social media referrer to websites was Facebook, with a global average of just 3.54 per cent.[10]

As the 2020s progress, and more and more time is spent on digital channels vying for our attention and time, there is perhaps good reason to start to reconsider other places to promote your travel business too. Direct mail, SMS marketing and TV ads have perhaps felt 'too expensive' or 'too old school' for most marketers to even think about when there are so many challenges in keeping up with the latest digital marketing movements and just getting through the to-do lists. However, with so many travel companies doing the same thing and increasing competition and costs in the market, revisiting some of these 'offline channels' shouldn't be dismissed. We'll come onto this more in a later chapter, but, as has been said by many over the decades, 'When the world zigs, zag.' If your competitors are all doing the same thing at ever increasing costs, then there is definitely a reason to review the places that you market yourself.

One thing that is often overlooked when it comes to digital media is the value of the placements that are made. You will know full well how annoying some of the adverts you see online are or just how terrible they can look. While it is easy to press some buttons and let Google and Meta create and distribute ads using AI in a matter of minutes, that doesn't necessarily mean that they are any good. Many a time we have shared examples of our clients or competitors inside our agency where the adverts just haven't been up to scratch and have sometimes looked, well, awful. Grey fonts, poor images, terrible wording and placements on rubbish websites have not helped to position our clients' amazing holiday companies well.

We sometimes assume that Google, Meta and others will place our media messages on websites that are of good quality and relevant to our customers. However, these promises and assumptions are far too often broken. If we think about brand and associations hard enough, digital media is often a terrible choice to place the right message to our audiences. Does an AI generated advert popping under a YouTube video for six seconds saying 'Buy a holiday in Morocco. £1,995 for 7 days' really help to make our brand and trips memorable? Does it really convey our key messages? And, most importantly, do users associate poor ad placements with high-quality and high-value travel? It's a big stretch to think that they do.

There is a reason why luxury brands sponsor luxury events (e.g. the Wimbledon tennis tournament or F1) while budget or local brands stick up posters around towns or just put an A-frame board outside a shop. Where you decide to place your adverts and message, the media you use and who you associate with are all indicators to your potential buyer. If you want to be seen as a higher-quality travel business, then you need to link yourself to higher quality places. That often comes at a cost, but alignment is key.

Buyers, whether they are aware of it or not, make buying decisions based on a huge range of factors, most of which we're not even aware of half the time. The study of behavioural science (or behavioural economics) is a recent discipline aiming to give us more tools, ideas and visibility of things that can help us to make better marketing decisions through better under-standing of human behaviour. And with this, place should not be overlooked.

If you've never seen or heard of Rory Sutherland, perhaps one of the most well-known personalities in this area, then I wholeheartedly recommend you watch some of his videos. One of my favourites of his isn't even his own work but it delightfully outlines the importance of place when it comes to marketing. It involves showcasing an Australian comedy duo Hamish and Andy. In their video, they walk the streets of Melbourne as a dodgy pair of chancers, trying to get random passers-by to go to their exclusive 'Ed Sheeran Peep Show' in an underground bar in the middle of the afternoon for the cost of two Australian dollars.[11] After two hours and twenty-three minutes of asking dozens and dozens of passers to buy a ticket without any success, they eventually coax in a male and female couple to go downstairs and take a seat. Even on the way into the private show with perhaps the most famous singer songwriter of the last decade, they get incredibly nervous and twitchy about the whole affair. Why on *earth* would Ed Sheeran be playing in a dodgy-looking downstairs bar on a Friday afternoon for $2?! But he was! The lucky punters took a big gamble and got to see a once-in-a-lifetime show, albeit only 30 seconds long, from one of the world's biggest stars.

While our comedic friends very helpfully illustrate all four of our market-ing Ps in this video to some degree, for me it's the 'place' that really stands out. No one would ever think of putting Ed on a tiny stage in a medium-sized city in Australia. His place is on stage in stadiums around the world. The disconnect between where the product was expected to be and where it was was so vast, that no one would buy it (well they did in the end, but it took a *lot* of persuading!).

While we think that digital media is the place to best position ourselves, we have to be very careful about where we allow our adverts and messages to go. If we don't, our brand can easily turn into something that doesn't even get noticed by our target customers.

The final thing to say, particularly for travel companies in the UK but also in many other countries, is that the travel trade is often the go-to place to market. There are many travel companies I've spoken with that rely only or nearly exclusively on the travel trade to sell their tours. For some businesses this is absolutely the right thing to do! However, commercially this can pose a risk, as often it's just a handful of trade partners that generate most of your business. If these relationships are solid and reliable and have no chance of moving, then you could just simply carry on and continue to sell tours and make profit. For any company to be reliant on one or two partners for most of its revenue is a risk, and one that should be clearly understood and managed.

Perhaps you're reading this book because you work for a travel company that is now facing this situation! Hello and hang in there. You've made the right choice to buy this and continue to read. Bringing in new channels to market to help spread your risk and perhaps take sales from your competitors can only be a good thing.

Promotion

The final P is promotion. This can be thought of in many ways, but for the purposes of this book I will be focusing mostly on the messages that we're sending out to the world to get attention for our company and our trips. These can be divided into three main areas – owned, paid and earned. All of these should be thought about in terms of who you want to speak to and how your audience wants to be spoken to.

- **Owned:** These are communication channels that are ours and under our total control. Think website, email lists, social media channels and any videos that we might create. These are all coming from within our business, and being pushed into the world from the places that we control and own. With that being the case, we should always ensure that we have clear and consistent communications that are linked back to an overall message (some might call it 'brand message/vision/values') so that you can keep things simple and also make it easy for potential travellers to understand what you stand for.

- **Paid:** These are channels where we will need to pay some money to someone to help get our adverts and messages in front of people. These could be things like Google Ads or Bing Ads, boosted Meta Ads, YouTube prerolls or even influencer campaigns. But it also extends to more traditional things like printed magazine ads, billboard, promotional gifts or radio jingles. Basically, anywhere you've had to pay to get your message shared, then you'll be paying for that media exposure.

- **Earned:** This is a bit of a different one and often comes from where you've invested time and effort into the other two places to get noticed and therefore people come to you first or reference you as an expert or authority. Often, earned media comes from some of the places above, like social media or trade press or, if you're lucky enough, TV, radio or perhaps online video. For the latter options, you need to have enough reputation as a brand and/or individuals from your company with enough recognition and credibility to have that happen. My mind always goes to the likes of travel journalist, Simon Caulder from the *Independent* immediately. To get to Simon Caulder levels of notoriety in the UK takes a large amount of time and effort. However, being known in a specific niche of travel could be something to aim for, so that if it comes to ski or safari, journalists will know to go to you, and you will start to get mentioned. PR is just one part of the earned media effort but probably the largest and easiest to understand.

The 4Ps in action

Ok, that's quite a lot of theory – what about the practical side of things? How do you make these ideas come to life and how do you apply them to your travel business?

Before we get into some real-life examples, it's worth emphasizing here that while you can have a detailed and thorough understanding of the 4Ps of your own company, it's very easy to get things wrong. And the impact of doing so can be potentially huge. Just because you know these areas it doesn't mean that you know what to do with them.

Getting alignment across all 4Ps is necessary to keep your business aligned both internally but also to the outside world. Many years ago in my early career I was introduced to the importance of aligning your 4Ps with an international business coaching company called Shirlaws. One of their skilled coaches called Richard spent a morning talking through how having a grasp of these areas of your marketing and sales plan is important, but more importantly how to make sure you get them really right. Whatever our 4Ps are, they should be aligned as best as possible to make sure our offering is consistent and feels 'right'.

Let's take our Australian comics mentioned earlier. If we were running their peep show business, we *could* look at our 4Ps as outlined below.

Product: Ed Sheeran

Price: He'll do a quick show for you for $2. Who's going to turn down the chance to see one of the most famous musicians in the world for $2?

Place: A dodgy underground club on a Friday afternoon.

Promotion: An iffy-looking grifter making offers to random passers-by.

Things were misaligned very badly. While this is an extreme version of the point I'm trying to make, it does very clearly show how not getting things aligned can cause problems to your sales numbers (one sale in two hours isn't great)!

Let's make it a bit more relevant to your challenges. Look at say, hotels in the UK. There are hundreds of hotel brands with thousands of beds for people to choose from. OK, it's not quite *that* simple, as the destination that you're going to is going to dictate the hotel that you pick. But, with all things being equal, there will be plenty to choose from regardless of the city you're visiting.

If you were the marketing manager for a hotel brand, you'd want to try to understand how well the competition shapes up and how you could potentially find a gap to exploit. Let's take a look at an example by giving a very simple measure for each of the 4Ps for a selection of hotel brands, saying if they are targeting the upper, middle or lower part of the market. Whether a brand should or wants to target one end or another is a completely different discussion point entirely. For now, let's just look at what the customers perception of each brand might be. Take a look at Table 2.2. The arrows should be self-explanatory, but the asterisks indicate which of the four is the one you should lead with in terms of messaging outwardly. Citizen M, for example, has a fairly unique product which could perhaps be seen as upper end depending on your viewpoint. However, the way their product looks and feels (quirky and modern and with a 'café culture' vibe) is distinctive against all of its competitor set.

TABLE 2.2 Perception of hotel brands in the UK, judging where they pitch their brand against the 4Ps

	Product	Price	Place	Promotion
Travelodge	→	↓	→*	→
Premier Inn	→*	→	→	→
Hilton	↑*	↑	↑	↑
Citizen M	↑*	→	→	→
Best Western	→	→	→*	→
Hotel Du Vin	↑*	↑	↑	↑
Britannia	↓	↓*	↓	↓

The idea of this task is to quickly try to see how they are positioned against the 4Ps and to see how they have (or haven't) differentiated themselves against what is an incredibly crowded market. Look at the Premier Inn, for example – they have spent a good chunk of their comms in recent years promoting the comfort of their beds and positioning their product above others in the market, while keeping other areas similar to the past. Is it truly upper end or luxury? Not really in the grand scheme of things, but it is something to push to be distinctive.

If in the traveller's head, they are able to get a better product against competitors while other areas are equal, then that gives the potential guest a reason to pick them over someone else. Hotel Du Vin purposely positions itself as a luxury hotel brand in the market – even the name suggests something out of the ordinary! If you went to stay at a HDV and the cost was shown as £79 on a hotel listing website, you'd think that something was surely amiss. Similarly, if they charged £200+ for a night but you turned up and found a broken lift and nails in your bed then you'd be immediately put off for life and no doubt tell all of your friends.

Hotels are perhaps a subjective example, given that you will always be limited by the place that you visit and if that hotel operates in your destination.

We could've looked at airlines as another option, but again, it's a similar story. I probably won't go out of my way to pick an airline if it means an extra four hours on my round-trip.

For you, though, the chances are that you will be selling online and will be up against a number of different competitors offering the same or very similar trips. The chance for the customer to pick you over your market is probably pretty equal on the surface. If you're in the search engine listings or in the magazines/websites that your potential traveller visits, then you're in with a shot.

Therefore, it's worthwhile spending some time to build out a table like Table 2.2 for yourself and perhaps half a dozen of your competitors. These competitors should be the ones that you know of from speaking to your customers (who else are you talking to about your trips?) but also some that you might not know who pop up on Google Ads, organic listings, social media searches or anywhere else you think your ideal traveller is going to spend time.

As mentioned earlier and throughout this book, the chances are you probably can't change many or any of these Ps I've outlined due to limited amounts of influence that digital marketers tend to have. Marketing's role is more often than not limited to the promotion and place part of the equation. Our ability to change price and product tend to be limited. However, it's worth putting them down in a table just to ensure that:

1 You understand your own place in the market.

2 You ensure that your board/directors are also clear on where you sit in the market too.

The key thing here is *alignment*.

Summary

It's more than OK to be one the cheapest in the market and offer a travel experience that is limited in some areas, if that's your marketing and sales strategy. It has worked very well for many brands. Just look at Ryanair! They revel in the fact that they offer the most basic of service at a cheap price. These businesses have turned over billions of pounds over the years but have a very definite position.

If you end up matching your competitors and market a lot of the time, then your next step is to pick one of these things to major on. Do you have a loud and charismatic leader? Make promotion your number one thing. Do you have amazing relationships with your supply chain? Perhaps price can be your number one? Do you know certain countries and cities better than almost anyone else? Product can be your friend.

Picking apart your market and own business using this framework can help you see things from the customer perspective, give you reason to push harder against your internal teams to do better or differently, or just help you get clarity about where you need to invest more to make a difference to your marketing results.

Notes

1 The Pokémon Company International. Pokémon GO exceeds 500 million downloads worldwide, Pokémon, 7 September 2016. press.pokemon.com/en/pokemon-go-exceeds-500-million-downloads-worldwide (archived at https://perma.cc/6SNQ-5D72)

2 T Dave. 'Pokémon GO' has lost 79 per cent of its paying players since launch, but that's fine. *Forbes*, 13 September 2016. www.forbes.com/sites/davidthier/2016/09/13/pokemon-go-has-lost-79-of-its-paying-players-since-launch-but-thats-fine (archived at https://perma.cc/NV9Q-HPAG)

3 The Marketing Centre. Marketing maturity in 2024: More than half of UK SMEs are marketing in the dark, The Marketing Centre, 2024. www.themarketingcentre.com/blog/marketing-maturity-in-2024 (archived at https://perma.cc/X5ZT-75Y2)

4 N Jakob. Why you only need to test with 5 users, NN/g, 18 March 2000. www.nngroup.com/articles/why-you-only-need-to-test-with-5-users/ (archived at https://perma.cc/KKB8-XWE6)

5 M Seaman. The right number of user interviews, Medium, 28 September 2015. medium.com/@mitchelseaman/the-right-number-of-user-interviews-de11c7815d9 (archived at https://perma.cc/UY4A-D2CD)

6 M Mason. Sample size and saturation in PhD studies using qualitative inter-views, *Qualitative Social Research*, 11 (3), 24 August 2010. www.semanticscholar.org/paper/Sample-Size-and-Saturation-in-PhD-Studies-Using-Mason/c25951ef3d0056c6fe63de9c920ff553e172eb8a (archived at https://perma.cc/4DCD-PDSE)

7 BBC News. Market research and the primitive mind of the consumer, BBC, 2011. www.bbc.co.uk/news/business-12581446 (archived at https://perma.cc/FKU5-YYDT)

8 IIMA Archives. Neil H. Borden – marketing, IIMA Archives, nd archives.iima.ac.in/faculty/Neil-H-Borden--Marketing-.html (archived at https://perma.cc/YN5C-2QPE)

9 Expedia Group Partner Central. The path to purchase, Expedia, 2023. partner. expediagroup.com/en-us/resources/research-insights/path-to-purchase (archived at https://perma.cc/N3XC-LM6A)

10 R Fishkin. Who sends traffic on the web, and how much? New research from Datos and SparkToro, 11 March 2024. sparktoro.com/blog/who-sends-traffic-on-the-web-and-how-much-new-research-from-datos-sparktoro/ (archived at https://perma.cc/NV7L-7TLV)

11 R Sutherland. Rory Sutherland's full speech @ Creativity4Better 2019 Conference, YouTube, 2019. youtu.be/E8-4JliHzoc (archived at https://perma.cc/38FZ-Y7DA)

3

Your digital channels of choice

Introduction

We've already looked at how the digital landscape has become de facto when it comes to marketing for travel brands. If it wasn't then you probably wouldn't have bought this book! But, despite this, not all travel businesses rely on digital marketing to meet their business needs. For some, traditional digital channels like search engine optimization (SEO) and increasingly pay-per-click (PPC), aren't suitable for them. Either the demand in search for their specific audience is too small or the costs are too much that it's not going to be profitable.

But most travel brands rely heavily on PPC, SEO, social media, email and other digital outlets to generate their bookings and keep growing their businesses. It seems like a crazy thing to even contemplate owning a travel business today and not employ the digital channels we all use every day to build your travel company.

But before we start looking into each of the channels, we do need to step back and look at our marketing (and business) plans to make sure that we pick the right ones to achieve our goals. So many times, we've seen travel companies just doing things because they thought they were 'supposed to' or because they 'always have'. This ends up with marketing teams looking at the wrong measures, completing the wrong tasks or, most worryingly, relying almost solely on one channel to deliver all their targets. When one channel delivers 80 per cent of your bookings, you must ask if your business is working for itself or the channel in question (too often Google)?

Selecting the right channels for your travel company at the start is fundamental to long-term success, as is evolving their use and focus over time.

Your digital marketing channel toolbox

Having started in digital marketing in 2003, I've seen the evolution of 'digital' as a channel. From something that was very niche and only really understood by 'techies', to now being almost the only way that marketing is done for many, the rate and scale of change has been phenomenal. It's now at a point where I must ask, what even *is* digital marketing? The phrase itself has almost lost meaning. If everyone spends nearly all their spare and working time online and nearly all marketing budget is spent with online platforms, then isn't it just… marketing? We don't really need to make the distinction between digital and offline marketing channels. Marketing is marketing regardless of the platform. And with many 'traditional' channels like out-of-home or radio ads being bought via large digital platforms, the lines between old and new marketing are becoming increasingly blurred. Everything has a digital interaction or influence within it somewhere.

The main distinction we'll make here for the sake of simplicity is that a digital channel is a separate way that a travel brand could get in front of a potential traveller, through a screen that the individual controls, as opposed to a screen that they might see around them, either in the home or out of it.

There are many different digital channels that we could use to help us influence and sell more holidays. Table 3.1 lists them in a pros and cons format, also noting whether they are for primarily short- or long-term goals.

This is the list as it stands currently. Over time, things have changed and they will change in the future. There is no doubt that the next few decades will bring in other channels that will shake things up again. Will we all be speaking to our AI agents in the 2030s to make our travel plans? No doubt some will be, in fact some might be now! But until it goes 'mainstream' it probably isn't worth thinking about, given just making the above work is usually more than enough to be getting on with.

Whether a channel should be considered or not can sometimes be decided using an incredibly complex process called the Mum Test. Actually, there is nothing complex about it at all, and it goes like this – if you show your mum something new, does she quickly understand it, and can she use it easily? You can also carry out a Dad Test, of course. I remember when I first showed Google to my parents they were quite amazed about what it could do! But not only did they understand it quickly, they also then adopted it quickly and could use it without my help. (It seems a crazy thing to say, but many people considered computers to be 'complex' things in the early 2000s.)

When the Google Cardboard virtual reality (VR) beta came out in the mid-2010s, again I showed my parents the art of the possible, where you

TABLE 3.1 Pros and cons of each digital channel

Channel	Platforms	Pros	Cons	Influence
Search engine optimization	Google, Bing	• Once top positions are reached, they can stay for months and years • Only cost is content creation and technical support • Clicks are 'free' and can be in large quantities in some instances	• Requires technical skill knowledge • Hard to show ROI on activities • Takes time to see results and lacks control due to algorithm changes	Mid/long-term
Pay-per-click	Google, Bing, Meta	• Can be turned on and off as required • Budget can grow over time if success is seen • Usually easier to see influence on bookings	• Auction-based, so costs tend to increase year on year • Google increasingly takes control over messaging and placement • Still needs expertise to get right	Short/mid-term
Social media (organic)	Meta (Facebook, Instagram), X	• Can reach massive audiences • Connect with travellers over a long period • Free to post	• Organic reach of posts is largely dead so need to spend money • Time is needed to create 'stand out' creative • Attribution is incredibly hard	Short- and long-term
Social media (paid)	Meta (Facebook, Instagram), X	• Better chance of reaching specific audiences than organic posting • Good control over messaging	• Needs ongoing investment • Needs some expertise to set up campaigns correctly • Doesn't usually translate into direct bookings	Short- and long-term

(continued)

TABLE 3.1 (Continued)

Channel	Platforms	Pros	Cons	Influence
Video content	YouTube, TikTok, Instagram	• Directly shows the product and traveller experience • Longer watch time possible • Can reach thousands if successful with algorithm	• Cost to travel to and then create video assets • Unless proactively promoted, unlikely to get large view count • Typically harder to prove ROI	Long-term
Email		• Data is owned by you • Still seeing 30% open rates in general • Low cost to send each time	• Spam filters increasingly pushing emails from inboxes • Apple and others removing tracking, making ROI harder • Lists need to be proactively built, which can take years	Short- and long-term
Display	Google, Meta	• Good levels of audience targeting • Visual media shows off product nicely • Can help keep the brand in travellers' minds	• Typically low to no ROI • Placement is increasingly hard to manually manage and quality is lower • Adblockers often stop display ads loading	Long-term
Chat	WhatsApp, Messenger, SMS	• One-to-one medium, so can be very personalized • Under-used channel, so high engagement rates • Integrations into other systems on increase	• Can get 'lost' in inboxes easily • Can be fiddly to set up • Attribution can be hard to measure	Short- and long-term

could effectively create a VR experience using a mobile phone, some cardboard and two small lenses. 'Well, that is amazing! It's incredible! Have you seen this?' They were really blown away by what was possible with technology. But could they confidently use it when I went? Absolutely not. While it was a good single use case, it didn't ever catch on with my parents, so it failed the Mum Test – it was still slightly 'techy' and didn't offer anything other than a gimmick.

For me, any digital channel with mass appeal or reach needs to be as simple as possible to pick up and use. And then it needs to offer good utility for someone to invest in it, both financially but also to change habits. If it doesn't do all these things then it doesn't really matter how useful it is, it will usually only have a place in a niche.

Selecting the channels for you

There are many things to think about when selecting the channels that are going to be the focus of your digital marketing plans. And, as I've said, they will and *must* evolve over time as the world, travellers' needs and technology changes.

Whatever channels you pick must be aligned to your business and marketing goals. Without these, then you're just going to be picking activities and tasks based your own expertise, skills and beliefs rather than helping your business succeed in the coming years.

A company focusing on ultra high-net-worth travellers that doesn't want to sell in the next five years is going to take a completely different approach to one serving a mass market audience looking to exit in the next 24 months. It's important for you in your marketing role to get as much visibility and knowledge of the wider company plans as you can. We must use the very finite resources that we have to make the best marketing bets and then stick with them to make sure that there is enough time to collect data to then make better decisions in the coming months and years ahead.

Table 3.1 illustrates why you might want to pick certain channels over the others based on what your short-term goals are. There is an argument that you should probably be using all of them to varying degrees, and I think there is *some* merit in that. No travel company really wants to rely solely on Google PPC to attract their customers. You're completely beholden to Google and your competitors for what happens to your success.

It would therefore make sense to spend some time on social media as well, right? Well, yes. However, the trap then is saying yes to social media with Facebook. And then Instagram. And then TikTok. And then video advertising because, why not? Within a few months, you've spread your budget very thin, you've spread your time across multiple platforms and your tracking is giving lots of misreading because you don't really know what channel delivered what.

Saying no to certain things is perfectly fine if that's the right move for your marketing efforts. Often, the bigger challenge is dealing with the internal politics that come with doing that. There will never be a perfect answer for the question of what the 'right' channels are for you or your business. There will always be a wide range of things to consider, but as I've tried to say here it's better to use fewer channels very well than to spread yourself too thinly across too many. At its heart, strategy is about deciding what not to do as much as what to do.[1]

The question that you really need to think about is how important your long-term goals are in comparison to your short-term ones. OK, everyone has passenger or revenue numbers to hit in the year ahead. And maybe you have one for next year too. But what about three or five years' time?

Obviously, knowing what the world will be like in five years is almost impossible to know. Just look at the last five years – few would've predicted a global lockdown, big shifts in geopolitics and such incredible hype around AI. But they happened. And other big changes could occur in future. So being too focused on the long term probably isn't going to be beneficial, as there are simply too many variables at play.

However, having some sort of idea of the scale you want to achieve in the longer term is important. If you want to perhaps double your turnover over five years, then that could be doable organically, using lots of short-term tactics to win travellers each year. You could then let rebooking rates build a large chunk of your growth over time if you have the product to sell them.

If you want to be four times the size then your approach needs to be quite different, as the chances are your easily accessed markets (via PPC) aren't going to deliver what you want. You will need to start to build more of a 'brand' to try to create mental awareness and availability in the head of your potential travellers. You need to keep an eye on medium-term trends about destinations, length and types of trips, and try to be ahead of these as much as you can. You should probably invest in some 'traditional' media to again build awareness. You'll need to invest in a much wider range of tactics and get your team to have lower expectations about short-term growth and return on investment (ROI) with a view to building over time. I know for most marketing directors or chief marketing officers (CMOs) this balance is incredibly hard. Pressure comes from chief finance officers, managing directors and board executives who all want to show revenue and profit now, and have confidence that things are 'working'. This pressure and reliance on 'spreadsheet culture' has created an incredibly tough set of conditions to operate in. The average length of time a CMO stays in post is roughly 40 months, as last reported in 2020,[2] which is reportedly the lowest of all board level roles.[3] Unless you have a supportive board to work with who understand your challenges, are aligned and are patient to get the results they want, then you're very likely to be under the 40 months count.

Getting the clarity about what the business objectives are will help you pick the best channels to increase your chance of success both for you personally and your company. Once you've identified these, you must then explain your thinking and rationale to those above you so that they too understand your plans and can buy into them and support them when times get tough.

What to do for each channel

Ok, so now you've got your channels selected. You have your targets for the year ahead and know what you need to do in the longer term. What do you need to make them happen? It's time to take a deeper look at each channel and understand the mechanics behind each one to make them work for you. The big focus for this book is to make your marketing more effective and to help you achieve your own personal goals as well as helping the business you're in to be more profitable. Strategy and channel selection is crucial when it comes to making your plans work and for you to be successful.

While the specific tactics and trends might change over time on each channel, there are some fundamental elements that each channel is built on that haven't really changed. In over twenty years of doing digital marketing at various levels of budget and travel focus, I think only social media has undergone a big change in terms of 'what works'. But we'll cover that more in the coming pages.

Search engine optimization

Background

When search engines were first created in the mid-1990s, the world was a different place. The internet was very slow, websites broke very easily, and unless you knew what website you wanted to visit you had no chance of finding anything. Directory listings akin to the UK's *Yellow Pages* printed telephone directory were built online to try to give users a chance of navigating to new and useful destinations. Search engines were built as a solution to the problem. Rather than scan down a list, why not have a text-based search box which 'knew' about the internet at large and then returned an answer to your query.

In 1998, Sergey Brin and Larry Page created a search engine while at Harvard University which was more advanced than other attempts. The computer program (algorithm) they'd written was based around the academic publishing world, where one research paper would reference another as a source of credibility. The more references a paper had and the more it was cited by other writers, the more valuable it was deemed to be. But understanding every reference (or link) on the internet required a lot of data and processing to try to make sense of the content being created. Google, a word play on the number 'googol', which is a very, very large number, was chosen as their company name to try to emphasis the size of the problem they foresaw.

Using their algorithm called PageRank (named after Larry Page, not web pages as is often thought) they created a search engine which returned far more accurate information than its rivals at the time. They also believed that users should be able to get to information quickly, and so rather than create a search engine alongside a directory or news website (which was the standard at the time to generate income for the owners), they built the home page with a single search box and two buttons – one to search and one to just show the first result.

Within a few years of official launch the search engine was growing in popularity as more people got online, technical users pushed Google internally at organizations to deliver better information for their colleagues, and word of mouth spread. Google soon became the standard by which all other search engines were measured and within a few years Google was one of the biggest properties on the internet. Casual users, technical internet people and everyone in between liked the simplicity, fun and 'do no evil' approach of this new company.

By the mid-2000s in most of the Western world, Google was number one and it caused many companies to think 'Just how do I make sure my website shows up top of the list when someone searches for my products?' And so, search engine optimization (SEO) as an industry was born – the practice of changing a website to appeal to search engines and gain better rankings to get as much relevant traffic as possible.

A new breed of marketing agencies started cropping up and practising SEO as a new way to market, sometimes in a good way, sometimes using unethical (black hat) techniques. And, ever since, Google has had to constantly evolve the way its algorithms work to ensure that those who try to game the system don't get their reward, as well as gradually bending things to meet their own needs rather than users.

However, in the last two decades of observing Google and how they have behaved, the moral compass that they originally set has certainly been moved and changed many times, and not in the ways that usually help you or your business. More often than not, it's to help their business and profit margins.

With that said, users are typing and hitting search more than they ever have. In 2024, Google processed over *five trillion* searches, which was roughly 500 billion a month or 60 million searches per minute.[4] By anyone's standards, that is a *lot* of data and a *lot* of processing. How has Google managed to create a business so vast?

First, as mentioned earlier, Google has had the best search engine available for many, many years. Their advanced programming of their search engine (at one point they had more people with PhDs working for them than any other company in the world) has nearly always given users what they wanted. From the original ten blue links, to incorporating maps, images, videos and many other types of information, they've understood better than any other company how users want to find information and then presented it to them better and quicker than anyone else. They've also found many ways to stop those trying to game the system better than any other search engine, which has, for the most part, kept their results 'clean' and satisfied user demands.

The second reason is Google have been very innovative over the years. From one of the most advanced mapping tools available in Google Maps, through to Google's suite of productivity tools like Sheets and Drive, they've been able to reinvest into a plethora of areas to help keep users engaged with the brand, but more importantly provide more data to inform further monetization for the business.

There is no doubt that these tools have at one point or another been literally game changing. I can recall the first time I used Google Maps and being blown away at the speed, functionality and ease of use, which was groundbreaking. One of the first projects I ever worked on in my agency was a mapping tool and it was a very big and complex build, taking many months to get to work. To then see a few years later a tool which had mapped almost every point on earth and could load in milliseconds was quite the thing. However, as time has gone on, Google has seemingly spent less and less on innovation and more and more on trying to push its own products instead of others.

Using its effective monopoly power, it's been able to push out dozens of perfectly legitimate businesses in favour of its own listings and tools, and has been fined billions of dollars as a result. For them it's perhaps just the cost of doing business. For some businesses around the world, it's been catastrophic.

While I personally have had many issues with how Google has behaved, not only in the courts but with many other moves it has made, which has caused me not to use it much this decade, I'm in a very small minority.

This comes to the third point behind their dominance. The power of default. For Google, this is based around two things. The first is that, generally, most internet users are pretty lazy. We like things to be made easy for us in life and in the case of Google, once I've found something that works well, what is the point in changing it? By being good at providing answers and being the go-to brand for search (you now don't search for things, you Google them) they made every other search engine almost irrelevant.

Although Google became the default because of the superior product, they also became default because they paid to be so. During the last 20 years, Google completed agreements with many technology companies to ensure that they picked up as much search engine traffic as they could and block out competition. The biggest of these deals continues to be with Apple, who are currently paid upwards of $20 billion per year to ensure that Google is installed as the default on all new iPhones.

This was another reason why they purchased the Android operating system in 2005 and they then decided to give it away free to many mobile phone manufacturers. By giving mobile phone companies a more feature-rich, robust and customizable OS rather than invest millions into making their own, they were able to load more Google products into devices and again keep their market share safe.

However we slice it, Google has been number one for several reasons and will continue to try to keep its revenue safe. It's worth understanding the history here and the relationships that it has with some of its biggest competitors, which has created an environment that is very hard to destabilize. If you pick up this book in 2030, there is an incredibly high chance that Google will still be the only real game in town when it comes to search engines as we know them.

FIGURE 3.1 Money paid by Google to Apple to make Google search default on iOS

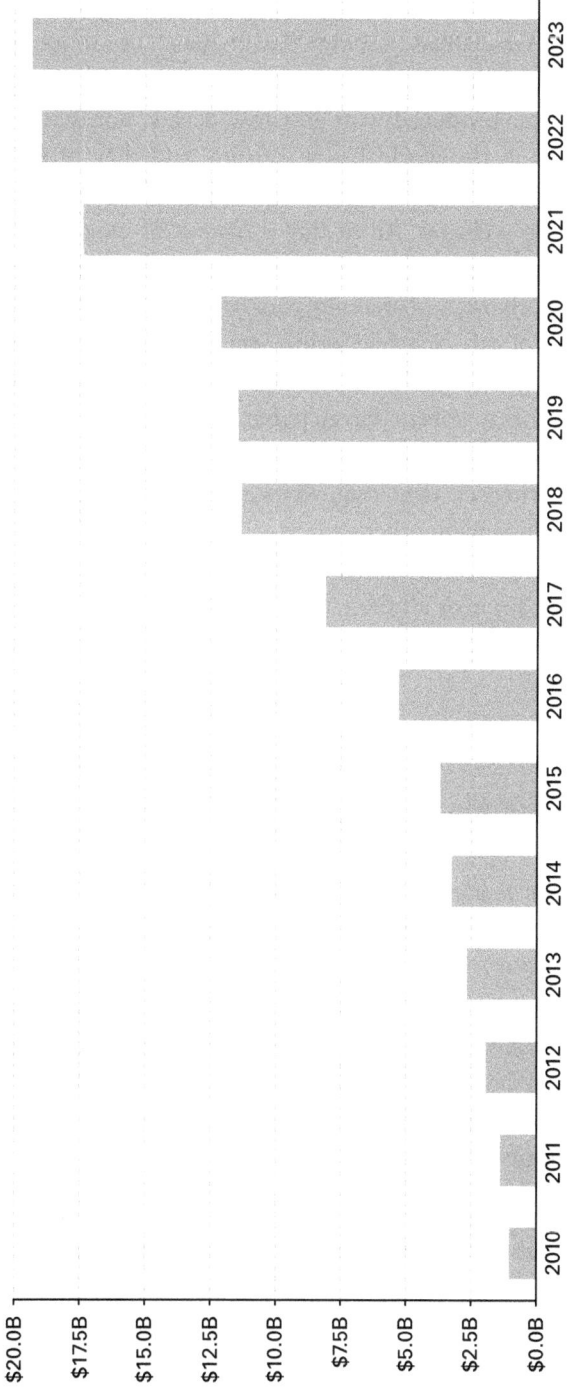

SOURCE Courtesy of Matthew Ball/Epyllion

SEO fundamentals

Google has had to change a lot over the decades. The internet in 2025 is very different to how it was in 2005. The amount of content produced each year is now what was produced with an entire decade not that long ago. Every travel business in the world has a website, and they often have multiple social media outposts as well as a wide variety of media available on video or image listing websites. All of this is on top of bloggers, publishers and online travel agencies (OTAs), which also produce mass volumes of content each day. The chances of making your website rank for the phrases you target sadly diminish each year unless you invest in your own SEO efforts.

With that said, the fundamentals of what search engines look for when it comes to ranking a website haven't changed. As mentioned earlier, Google started from university and applied the referencing model of academic papers to the internet. One long, well-researched piece, written by credible authors and referencing other sources of content, was the basis of how the algorithm works. And even today that model still holds. Therefore, you should aim for some or all these things within your website:

- You, your brand or perhaps the author of the content are recognized as an entity by others in your world.
- You reference other people of note or interest as places to further the knowledge of your reader.
- You present your information in a clear and presentable way, doing your best to address the needs and concerns of the reader as the primary focus.

Put another way, your job is to create really good content that perhaps no one else can or has before, present it in an easy-to-read manner, within a website that loads fast and is ideally referenced by other people.

To put that into specific activities for you, this means:

- Write content that is seen as *expert*, using your *experience*, is *authoritative* and *trustworthy*. This means writing content from your own team in a way that is unique but is first and foremost for your target readers. For a very long time, it was thought that content should be written for search engines first, rather than users, but Google has tried hard to prioritize and reward well thought out and unique content above anything else to help broaden its potential traveller's knowledge.

- We must also face the fact that in these modern times it is incredibly easy for AI tools like ChatGPT and many others to create content at scale at the touch of a button. Our company approach is 'If an AI could write it, then we shouldn't.' This doesn't mean you can't use AI to give you ideas, or start off content pieces – by all means do that. But it should *not* be used to create the bulk of your website content, as often it will just recreate content already in existence, make errors or not carry your own tone.

- When you write this content, make sure that from a technical (HTML) point of view, you put the main things you want the page to rank for or be seen for in the TITLE tag and Heading One (H1) and Heading Two (H2) tags, to make the signals as clear as possible about what the page is about. These can usually be easily updated in your CMS.

- Do *not* stuff the words you want to rank for in the body of the text in a way which is obvious or makes it hard for users to read. Use natural language as much as possible, but where you can weave in the phrases, words and entities that you think relate to the page, where appropriate.

- Ensure that your website is as error free as possible. Perhaps the best way to do this is by checking in Google Search Console (GSC) (which take a few minutes to set up if you haven't already) for errors that Google has flagged to you. GSC is there to help you identify areas of improvement, because ultimately it's in Google's interest to tell you where faults are, so that if you do end up being listed in the search engine results pages you don't give a bad experience to the person landing on your website. That ultimately could lead to a poor website experience, and in turn potentially give Google a reason not to list you.

- Do as much as you can to promote your travel business in other places online. While Google's original algorithms were built around finding and then following links from one website to another, as time went on they realized that link manipulation was a real problem. Website and links were created with the sole purpose of boosting website rankings, and further improvements were needed to their algorithm, which led to the addition of brand mentions on other websites being a ranking factor alongside links. While the exact value of links has been a discussion point over two decades, there is no doubt that they, and mentions of your brand and key people within it, all help to increase where you end up in the search engine results pages.

Planning your SEO approach

Each page on your website is an opportunity to rank for a specific phrase. It's important to split out your website so that you can make each page rank for a defined set of phrases as best you can, rather than making your home page or some category pages do all the hard work.

As an example, a client approached me once and wanted to promote his luxury car touring travel company which sold trips to different parts of Europe. They mentioned that they weren't seeing many enquiries coming in outside of email marketing, which was the main driver of their bookings. While this was fine, they weren't reaching new audiences, and they wanted to do this to grow their revenue and profitability.

Unfortunately, due to the way their pages were built, this was never likely to happen. They had listed all their tours on one long page with booking buttons under each tour to take users to a generic booking page. This wasn't only bad for the user experience (a booking form should ideally be specific to that trip you want to go on – don't make your users re-enter data!) but also for search engines too. As a 'blind' user, the search engine can only go on the clues that are contained within the page, and if there are 15 trips listed on one page, each to different places for differing costs and availability, you're not making it easy for the search engine!

We recommended to the client that some work should be done to the website to make it easier for search engines and users to find the specific trip they wanted to go on, which meant creating specific pages for each tour, with links to them from the main listing page. When the changes were made, their listings increased in many places, and they were able to pick up additional bookings.

For me, this is a straightforward change, but if you don't think about your website from an SEO perspective, it's one that is missed and results in fewer opportunities for growth.

But what pages should be built and what should they contain? Ideally, this planning phase, known sometimes as the keyword research phase, should be done *before* a website is built, rather than after. Understanding the words which are relevant to your market and, ideally, what competition there is for each of them, can help to make better bets when it comes to your SEO efforts. There is no point in trying to rank for a popular phrase when some of the biggest travel brands in the world are already there. Similarly, there is no point in ranking for a phrase that is only searched 10 times a month.

What is right or wrong? Sadly, there is no right answer here. Each website, marketing budget and market is going to be different and so I can't give specific advice here. There is a certain art to keyword selection and knowing what is achievable. It can take many years to master what to target and why. If you've not done this before then don't worry about getting it wrong – the main thing is that you're doing it! If I had a pound for every website that went live only to then realize that their rankings have declined or disappeared, well, then I'd have lots and lots of pounds! Many companies focus on the aesthetic of the design and templates, which is undoubtedly important. But for most travel companies, Google is their biggest and best website visitor and so we need give them as much as we can to help them give back to us.

It's worth noting that keyword research numbers can only really come from a few places, either Google itself or some tools which have access to large datasets via internet service providers (ISPs). Both are prone to data issues where numbers aren't 100 per cent accurate; Google will 'round' data to make things less clear or obvious, and ISPs will be getting data via virtual private networks (VPNs), third party providers and other places, which often makes it full of holes. However, there aren't any other options, and we need to use what we can to piece together a plan.

A KEYWORD RESEARCH EXAMPLE

Let's say you sell adventure holidays in the UK. You could use Google Keyword Planner (only available with a Google Ads account) and search for not only the phrase 'adventure holidays uk' but all the different types of holidays you sell. The list that would come back from Google's Keyword Planner would look something like Table 3.2.

TABLE 3.2 Example of Google Keyword Planner monthly searches

Keyword	Avg. monthly searches
adventure holidays	9,900
adventure holidays 2025	50
adventure holidays 2026	40
adventure holidays adults	590

(continued)

TABLE 3.2 (Continued)

Keyword	Avg. monthly searches
adventure holidays couples	320
adventure holidays for families	2,400
adventure holidays uk	1,600

This isn't meant to be an exhaustive list, it just illustrates the point that a 'core' term ('adventure holidays') can and will have many, many variants which need to be considered. Each of these variants will also often have vastly different search volumes and intents. It's important to acknowledge these and have an understanding that some phrases will be more popular with searchers. That doesn't necessarily mean that they should be selected for your SEO efforts, though.

You must ask yourself two questions – first, is this phrase really aligned to my travel business and products? If you sell adventure holidays for couples and adults but don't for families, then it's not worth chasing that phrase even if it has five times more searches per month. The second thing to try to understand is how realistic it is going to be to rank for that phrase. Just entering that search into Google and scanning down the list will show if they are all your main competitors or not. What is the chance of you outranking them? If the top three or four spots are taken by big travel brands, then it's probably not worth pursuing. Google has always favoured bigger brands and it could take you many years to get anywhere near them. However, if those positions are filled by companies of your size then it could well be achievable in a reasonable timeframe.

Ultimately, I'd recommend getting an experienced freelancer or agency who has done this type of exercise many times before to help you here, as this keyword research exercise should really inform your SEO efforts for at least 12–24 months. Getting it correct is worth the investment, as doing it on the cheap or not at all (as is sadly the case in far too many instances) will only lead to more wasted time and effort in the future, and perhaps a thought that 'SEO doesn't work', when it is poor execution rather the channel itself which is the issue.

The final point to emphasize here is that once you've narrowed down your list of phrases you want to target, you should then be clear about which page on your website you want Google to rank when they search for that phrase. No doubt you already have a website, so it's important to take stock of the pages you already have and see if you have multiple pages that could potentially rank for that phrase.

Let's say you had a page on your website targeting 'adventure holidays for couples' but then you also had a blog called 'the top adventure holidays for couples'. Which page should Google rank? It could be that these pages are incredibly similar in terms of content, structure and focus, and so you're creating an issue for yourself where you're making it hard for Google to know what page to rank. The most likely outcome is that neither will! You should probably keep your main product page as the key focus and then edit your blog to focus on something like 'the top adventure holidays in 2027'. With some content, heading and page name updates you could shift the focus towards future bookers rather than the current day ones. This would create a clear delineation between the two pages and then allow Google to understand which one to rank and for what phrase.

There are many other areas of SEO that are worth investing and spending time reading up on if you want to increase your SEO footprint. I believe that these are the basic things that every digital marketer should understand and have some ownership of. It is important to understand technical areas of website set-up and speed, but even by Google's own words it's worth bearing in mind that making your website slightly faster is highly unlikely to make any dent in your rankings.

The most overlooked part of SEO: Your home page

My final point to think about with SEO, which applies equally to any channel, is the page that you'd like to rank for will nearly always be the first page that your potential travellers see of your company. And after looking through hundreds of Google Analytics accounts over the years, my estimate is that of everyone who lands on a product or category page from SEO or PPC, only 10–20 per cent of them will see your official home page. It's usually a very small number, and is a huge opportunity missed.

One of the biggest tricks that the digital marketing profession has missed over the last decade is just this. The best offers, best products and best badges of trust are nearly always kept just for the home page, which is typically visited by people who've typed in your brand name and so already know who you are! You shouldn't need to influence these people, they already know you! What about those that have no idea about you and find you from a generic search? *These* are the ones you should be trying to win over!

If you want to really maximize your conversions from your SEO and PPC efforts, then you need to design your SEO pages (and templates) to really shout about your travel brand, why you're so great and different to your competitors. Any badges of credibility, offers or messages you want to convey should be rippled through your target landing pages and not just your home page, as they just won't be seen!

If you take nothing else from this section, please remember that *every website page is a potential home page.*

Pay-per-click (search ads)

If you're going to continue to answer over five trillion searches per year, then you need to generate some income to pay for all that set-up! Google are able to, with perhaps one of the biggest ever money machines that humanity has ever seen – Google Ads. When Google first came to attention in the late 1990s, they had the best search engine in the world, and it grew fast. But without a business model to support the company, they needed to come up with ideas to attract more investment to help them scale. Other search engines were as or more popular at the time, with the likes of Yahoo!, AltaVista, Excite and others leading the way. But their approach was to offer more than search by adding news, sport, weather and lots of other content on the home page. They made their money from large take-over ads and search was more an additional part of the offering, rather than the central one.

Google needed ideas to generate income. In 1998, their competitors in the search space were primarily focused on other features outside of search. Except one. That company GoTo.com, ended up changing the world, albeit indirectly. The owners of GoTo.com knew that spam and bad content were likely to show up in the search results (even then!) and knew that some phrases had real commercial value. Using a tried-and-tested model borrowed from the likes of the *Yellow Pages* and others, where business would pay to put their name next to certain categories, they offered the same. When a user typed in a certain phrase, GoTo.com would allow a business advert to appear at the top of the listing, thus pushing spam further down the page and giving business owners the chance to put themselves in front of potential customers.[5]

There was no real copyright to this idea as it had been used many times over many decades. After a few initial attempts at building their own version as well as potentially partnering with GoTo.com (by this time called Overture), Google launched Google AdWords in 2002 in the US as a self-serve platform which eventually made it to the UK in late 2003.

And so, Google AdWords, now Google Ads, was born. The company skyrocketed from scrappy Silicon Valley start-up to one of the biggest and most profitable businesses in the world. The cash made from Google Ads then allowed them to scale into other areas of business but to this day still makes up vast majority of their income and profit (something like 60–70 per cent per year out of roughly $300 billion per year). As it is so important to them, they are always finding new ways to squeeze out just a few percent extra per year to keep the markets happy and profit coming in.

The scale and size of the revenue generated by Google is still quite hard to fathom. A global business that generates 60–70 per cent gross profit on hundreds of billions of dollars year after year is quite the achievement. It's so embedded into how we do business now that the competition has had to follow the lead of Google, as for most countries it's the only option available when it comes to search.

With that said, it's worth quickly mentioning Microsoft's Bing. Market share in most Western countries varies between low single figures and 10 per cent depending on where you are in the world. While it's never going to change how you market your travel business, it is worth at least a small investment. Creating a campaign in Bing Ads is pretty much the same as it is in Google Ads and you can even copy and paste your Google set-up across. It's almost no hassle to get going and often the users on Bing will be slightly more affluent and slightly older. If you want to reach this type of audience, then it's worth trying to get 100 per cent of the opportunity available, as it could well produce better results albeit on a much smaller scale.

Google Ads fundamentals

While Google has continued to shift various goalposts over the years with SEO to keep ahead of spammers and ensure their own products are as visible as possible, the fundamentals of PPC haven't changed a lot.

Back when Google AdWords first launched, the idea was to create the most targeted adverts you could towards the specific phrases typed in by your potential travellers. That is still the case now. If you want to sell 'adventure holidays to couples' and 'adventure holidays to solo travellers' then you can do that. If you were to do this with an SEO mindset, you'd build two distinct pages and content targeting those specific audiences.

In PPC, the exact same principle applies, but instead of website pages, you would build out a group (called ad group) within the Ads interface and then theme as much as you could around that specific focus. Each ad group should contain the specific set of phrases to target which are relevant and as all-encompassing as you can think without going too vague. You can also define the specific text to show to the user when that phrase is shown (known as adtext) as well as a specific landing page. All of this is shown in Table 3.3, which outlines how two different traveller types can be targeted.

Each phrase should have its own maximum that you want to spend on it when a user clicks on it, known as a cost per click (CPC). Some phrases will be commercially more important and relevant than others both within each ad group and compared to other ad groups that you want to create. By setting higher CPCs for phrases over others, you're dictating where your targets are.

As well as setting up the phrases that you want to target for a specific theme, you can also say the words and phrases that you *do not* want to match against. These are called negative lists and ideally each ad group should have a set of words that you do want to appear for (e.g. 'cheap' or 'free').

Sadly, as time has gone on, Google has done more and more things to try to be 'helpful' and match your ads to more and more things. This in turn means more and more irrelevant phrases get matched, clicked on and are spending your budget unless you proactively exclude words and phrases over time. A good negative list for your group is essential to ensure your focus remains narrow and on the phrases that add value.

The final principle about ad groups is that you have the control to set each one separately from each other. This includes a budget for each as well

TABLE 3.3 Example Google Ad set-up for two different themes

	Couples	Solo
Headline 1	Couples adventure trips	Best adventure for you?
Headline 2	Adventure trips for both	Your next adventure solo?
Description 1	Want an adventure trip for you and your partner? We're experts in adventure trips for two	Our adventure travel experts have helped thousands of solo travels explore the world
Description 2	We offer the best couple trip planning and have great deals to book now!	Our team are experts in solo travel and have great deals to book now!
Final URL	www.travelco.com/adventure	www.travelco.com/solo

as the targeting options. Let's assume that a couples booking is worth more to you than a solo traveller. It'd make sense to spend more money on that one than your solo group. Therefore, you could set a maximum ad group spend of say £20 per day for that group versus £10 for the solo one to ensure that you spend more on the audiences and products that you want to sell more of.

Adding extra layers to your Google Ads groups

As time has gone on, we've been given more layers to put on top of basic keyword targeting which are often underused. When it comes to making your Google Ads campaigns perform to their peak, adding as much information as you can into the mix is always beneficial and can help your campaigns rise above the competition.

I know for a fact that most PPC campaigns don't use these tools, and this is an opportunity for you. Here is a quick list of things that you should consider adding to your ad groups campaigns to make them find that extra few per cent in performance:

- Audiences and demographics: You can target your ads at different people who search for the phrases you set up, not just words. An audience can be pulled from your Google Analytics account (if set up) or can be done in Google Ads itself to target users based on age, gender or location. If you know that people have been onto your website and clicked book but not completed a booking, or you know they reside in a particular part of your country or the world, you can home in on those specific people (e.g. increasing your bids) and increase your chances of hitting your marketing goals.

- Time: People have busy lives and, depending on their stage in life, will be doing tasks at different times of the day. Targeting parents with young children is quite different to targeting solo travellers who are in their 70s. If you can understand this then you can use it to your advantage and bid differently at different times of the day and different days of the week. It might be best to bid more for younger families between 9pm and 12pm at night, when their children are in bed and they get a few spare hours to search for a break, while targeting an older generation could benefit from increasing bids during the daytime, when perhaps they have more time to look around. You should test your theories based on the personas that you create (as mentioned in Chapter 2) and see if they hold up and there is benefit from changing your bids.

- Bid strategies/type: Certain campaigns might have different objectives to others. For some people that you want to reach, they might not be in place to book just yet and so just being in front of them will be enough. For others, you might want to get them to book now. Google knows this and a lot about the people who search and offers several bidding types to cater to your needs. We can now set up our groups to target *return on ad spend* (how much you want to spend in percentage terms in order generate a certain amount of revenue) or *cost per acquisition* (how much you want to pay in monetary terms to get a booking or lead) as well as maximizing the number of clicks or conversions that you might want. Choosing the right bidding strategy for the right group and phrases requires a good level of thinking and understanding of how Google Ads works but in the right hands can offer incremental benefits to how your budget is spent.

Planning your Google Ads campaigns

Let's assume that you already have a Google Ads campaign running. Most of the travel businesses I've worked with have a Google Ads campaign either live now or on pause for some reason (i.e. being out of season, perhaps new marketing people coming into the team – that could be you!). If you don't have a Google Ads campaign running, then you're likely to be in the minority.

Like SEO, the key thing to remember about PPC planning is that it needs to be as granular as possible. The approach hasn't really changed in the last two decades. Understand your products and understand the keywords that are being used using the Google Keyword Planner, then map out the two things. The question is, which phrases should be grouped together? Which landing page should they end up on? And what do you need to say in your adverts to entice potential travellers to click? It should be that simple as a start.

The bigger question should then be to understand the value of each of those groups and/or clicks. Is it worth bidding more for family trips versus solo? Are certain countries or trips more profitable than others? If some are, then it might be worthwhile spending more per click to invest in bookings that will generate more profit for your company. The likelihood, though, is that other travel companies will also be doing the same as you and bidding against you. PPC ads are placed on the page in 'ad rank order' which is largely made up of the original bid per phrase and the quality of the campaign set-up. If we assume your competition have done an OK job of setting up their ads, then budget will be a deciding factor as to how you rank against them. It will then come down to how aggressive you want to be with your bids to decide where you end up in the listings against them.

TABLE 3.4 Example cost per click estimates from Google Keyword Planner

Keyword	Average monthly searches	Competition	Average cost per click
adventure holidays	9,900	Medium	£1.43
adventure holidays 2025	50	Medium	£0.84
adventure holidays 2026	40	High	£1.99
adventure holidays adults	590	Medium	£1.48
adventure holidays couples	320	Medium	£1.17
adventure holidays for families	2,400	High	£1.87
adventure holidays uk	1,600	Medium	£0.95

There are two additional columns to the earlier table which are available when you use the Google Keyword Planner. These apply to the Google Ads auction *only*, not to SEO, which has several different factors around competition which can only be really seen using third party tools such as Semrush, Moz, Ahrefs, AWR and many others.

The competition and cost that you will face for each phrase is only indicative as the auction is real-time and Google has a habit of being vague with its predictions. While they are usually in the right ballpark, don't be surprised to see some or all of these numbers be anything from 20–40 per cent off from real world results.

That aside, here we can see that if we want to target families rather than a couple, there is a good opportunity for volume, with family phrases having almost eight times the amount of searches each month. This is great! We can sell more holidays! However, our costs are also much higher too (nearly 60 per cent per click) and competition is also greater, with more people in that specific auction. Therefore, we should expect our costs to be significantly higher now but also in the longer term, as with higher competition comes higher costs. Competitors are likely to push their bids up to get placed higher on the search pages, leading us to potentially do the same, and so on it goes.

My expectation is that you've already got real world data that you could investigate. Perhaps you have direct access to your Google Ads campaign or use a report which has been sent to you. Your job as a digital marketer is to understand where your budget is being spent and where you are getting the best results. The first point of target phrase selection is most definitely under your control. If you haven't selected the right phrases to begin with then you're going to struggle to get a good return on your spend. The analysis of whether this has worked is something that we'll look at later.

BEING STRATEGIC WITH PPC

How you see your PPC spend within your overall marketing plans and strategy is quite important. I think given that most travel businesses have been spending on Google Ads for many years, we sometimes forget what our intentions are with it. I have seen many clients spend hundreds of thousands of pounds a year but not truly know if it has delivered positive returns and what the value to the business is.

Far too often, a top-level report will be shared which might show an average CPA of, let's say, £100. This might be within the overall success metrics for the business, which could appear like a good thing. However, if you look deeper, you will likely see a few things. The first is that the Google Ads account contains a number of brand terms or matches to brand phrases by Google within some of its 'helpful' matching (i.e. trying to spend more budget more often if not tightly controlled). When a user searches for a brand, it usually means two things:

1 They know about the brand in advance and are therefore 'warmer' in terms of conversion, purely from the fact that they know who they are looking for.

2 They are perhaps much more likely to purchase or make an enquiry.

The behaviour of a brand click is usually quite different to that of a generic one. And so is the cost. Brand clicks are always the cheapest and highest converting. And most Google advertisers are not stupid. They know that it's not possible to get a conversion when someone clicks on a brand advert if they represent a different travel company and so don't usually bother to bid on your brand. Therefore, with less people in the auction, you will likely pay less for your click as well as seeing a much higher conversion rate.

Often it can be the case that a monthly spend of say £10,000 per month, might be generating CPA of £100 per customer for your travel business, which could be very fair value! The real devil in the detail, though, might show something like Table 3.5.

On a top level, all objectives are met. But, as you can see here, we're getting half of our conversions from less than 10 per cent of our spend, which is capturing people that already know about us. The numbers and averages are completely skewed due to cheap and highly relevant brand clicks blurring our picture. If we take these out, then our true CPA is more than doubled! If we want to grow our travel business, we must be realistic and work to a CPA of £200 (or more) for new bookings rather than the £100 that we are kidding ourselves about, and this is crucial to understand.

TABLE 3.5 Example of Google Ads reporting broken down by ad group

Ad group	Average cost per click	Monthly spend	Conversions	Cost per conversion
Brand	£0.43	£788.03	55	£14.33
Family trips	£2.88	£6,509.12	24	£271.21
Solo trips	£1.71	£2,764.33	20	£138.22
Total		£10,061.48	99	£101.63

The follow-on point here is that £200 may appear to be expensive in the short term; however, it will depend on how long-term your objectives are as to whether you can justify it. If you are looking to build your booking numbers over a longer period, let's say three to five years, then what you could argue you are doing in the current year is winning clients now at say a break-even rate, with a view to getting them to rebook several times in the coming years.

In this example, if we paid £271 for our family to book with us in year one, but they then travelled twice more over the next five years, our average cost per trip would come down to £90, below our £100 target, and therefore be profitable (and in real terms could be even lower in five years' time with inflation!). It is very simplistic to just expect a client to book twice without investing any more to bringing them back of course, as any marketing activity will incur at least some cost. Email, organic social media, text messages all cost money per send and/or time for someone to craft and manage. However, these costs will be significantly lower than Google's charges and so therefore don't really change our view too much.

How much you are prepared to pay should be very much aligned to your business goals and marketing strategy which have been created. You should always be clear on your intent. The reality is that, as time goes on, Google Ads become more expensive unless we change some other factors like our product, pricing or another one of our Ps from Chapter 2. If those levers can't be pulled then you must ask whether Google Ads is a viable option for your travel company, and if it is, understand which areas you can realistically afford to bid on. In our example here, if it costs £100 to win a new client and that is all we can afford to spend due to our margins, then strategically we'd have to turn off our family trips phrases. It would then be a case of working harder to get our costs down for our solo trips over time to stay within the profitability boundaries set by the business. It is crucial to understand the factors at play here to make sure that you make the best decisions for your business and that this is communicated properly internally.

Social media channels

Organic social media

We can't talk about digital marketing channels without talking about social media. It has fundamentally changed many things about society over the last few decades, from how we consume information and news to how we view ourselves and the world around us. For travel, the impact has been vast, as talked about in Chapter 1. Where once our destinations were curated by a few TV personalities or weekly print writers, now anyone with a mobile phone, small bit of money and confidence can help shape where, when and how we travel.

Every travel brand will have at least one social media account and will be posting several times per week or even per day. Social media is a crucial part of our marketing mix, with it influencing anything from just 3 per cent (see Chapter 4) to 75 per cent of travellers,[6] depending on the country or age profile of the people you interview. How much it matters to your specific business depend on the profile of who you want to target with your trips. Therefore, how significant it is to you is very much dependent on your business. What might be your main route to market might be someone else's outpost that gets very little attention. The hype around social media has been vast for a very long time and doesn't always translate into real world commercial benefits for many. For every brand or creator that has sold a million pounds' worth of holidays through Instagram, there are many hundreds of companies that get a handful of likes per post each week or have seen their engagement measures go down rather than up over time.

We can't have a prescriptive approach with social media as the rules of engagement change over time. In the early days of social media, we could only post images and text, and for many years this was a formula for success. Now, in the 2020s our organic reach is often in the small sub 1 per cent mark on average.[7] Over the last decade, as Meta and other platforms have battled to keep our attention, video has been the predominant format to engage users and keep them online for longer. For any brand wanting to engage with new and existing travellers, the main priority should be to create video content on an ongoing basis to showcase the destinations that you take people to. Sadly, for most marketers across the globe, this doesn't come naturally and takes up an incredibly large amount of time. In fact, it is the second biggest challenge when it comes to social media, as reported by We Are Social in 2025, second only to overall resource (time/people) available.[8]

With time and reach both limited, more and more marketers are turning to paid social options to try to meet their goals to try to cut through to their target markets. In Europe, nearly three out of four marketers now use paid social ads to promote their business, albeit on a small scale, with less than 5 per cent of their total spend going there.[9] Paid social channels can and should make up part of your marketing approach but not be the sole source of lead generation. Most users on social are there for their own reasons and not yours. And those reasons tend to stay fixed over time. We are social animals and so use these platforms to not only keep in touch with our friends and family but also to hear from people (like celebrities and influencers) we like and find interesting.[10]

Aside from that, social media is primarily used as an entertainment platform to rival traditional TV watching, both at home and on the move. The days of sitting idly in the departure lounge looking at planes taking off is now largely changed to people sat staring at the screen a few feet away from them and being taken to another world through YouTube, Netflix or TikTok. We do *not* use social to connect and communicate with friends, as was the mission for most platforms when they were originally created. In documents posted by Meta in their anti-monopoly trial in April 2025, they showed in court that only 17 per cent of Facebook and just 7 per cent of Instagram time spent on the platform was looking at friends' content.[11] The rest of the time was spent looking at content from brands or from people they didn't know. When up to 90 per cent of spent time on social media is anything but social, we know things have fundamentally changed.

Social media is an entertainment platform, and so we need to think of our travel company and the content we make ideally through this lens, too, to some degree. A stuffy, bland, non-conversational video of a hotel complete with generic acoustic strumming in the background is not going to compete against a guided tour from the local hotel manager talking about various amenities with the local staff in a vibrant atmosphere. Potential travellers want to be engaged and entertained so if we can offer at least some of that, then our chances of success will greatly improve. It's about showing real experiences, real stories and real insights into the places that you will take users and how they will feel when they get there. Travellers want to get as much of an idea as possible about where they will be going and what they will spend their hard-earned savings on, which is where social media *can* be your friend.

We know that things will change over time with these platforms, but there are some fundamentals that I think hold true now as much as they did

10 years ago. The specifics and dynamics will always move and there will always be new tweaks made as they try to keep users watching for as long as possible while squeezing a few extra pence out of advertisers each year:

- **Show some emotion!** Generic images and generic words are never going to go viral. Sadly, the world of social favours 'edgy' content to pull on our emotions and feelings and create debate about content. We can't all be posting like Ryanair (who are happy to play with their brand in a way most aren't), but we should be looking to at least create some emotion with our current followers and fans as well as new ones too. You don't like watching boring videos or follow boring accounts and your travellers don't want to either.

- **Video is more engaging than images:** Ever since the TV was invented, we've largely built our living areas around it at home. As humans, we want to watch moving things rather than static images, in the main. Images led the internet in the early days but that was largely due to technical constraints. Since broadband and 4G have reached most of the world, video has become a major part of the social web and should be your first port of call when creating content.

- **Post regularly:** You can't build a brand by showing up a few times a month, especially in a near-infinite sea of content. To get any sort of traction, both with your audience and the algorithms, you need to create content on a regular basis. What regular means to you is going to be down to how much time you have, what videos and imagery you can get hold of and other factors. But having a schedule of say 3–5 times per week is a good place to start. If you can't post regularly then your only other option is to go 'big' with your content, posting less often but with bigger and higher quality content. This could be high video production values or in-depth research into something relevant to your brand or travellers.

- **Don't have high expectations:** This might seem counterintuitive when nearly all digital media is quantifiable and measurable, but being too analytical about social media is sometimes a dead end. Social content should help to keep your brand in the traveller's mind, not necessarily make them book directly. They aren't going to be booking a trip every month with you, so expecting lots of bookings from each post is the wrong mindset. Sharing content from your own team or suppliers should primarily be there to remind your followers of the places you go, experiences you provide and any offers you have right now. Ultimately, it should inspire them into action *at some point*. In the UK, research from ABTA suggests that travellers take about four trips per year and these are of varying lengths and spend.[12] So if you sell high-end historical tours don't expect to sell to every person who follows you every year. Of course, there are always some travel companies who can say that social is one of their biggest drivers of success, but this is the exception rather than the norm.

- **Narrow your focus:** This applies to both the number of platforms that you post onto as well as types of content that you post about. In 2024, the average user has around seven 'social media' profiles (although this does include WhatsApp and YouTube, which are not 'social networks', I'd argue) but is usually only active on around five of them.[13] Depending on who your target travellers are should impact the focus of where and how you post. Unless you have huge resource and manpower, it's not possible to invest in all channels and we must be focused on who we want to speak to and where they hang out. Saying no is a good thing!

These are some hard-earned tips from me based on what I've seen other travel brands do over the last decade. Because social is increasingly more about media than connection, getting the right tone, video production and assets for your brand is hard. It becomes a lot to manage. Sometimes it becomes a real distraction and pain. But if you think of your social channels are a multimedia brand experience, then you're more likely to see success than just seeing it as something to do because every other travel company does.

Paid social media channels

You already know that social media has undergone some very big changes in the last two decades, evolving from a social first approach to more recently focusing on interests and entertainment. Travel brands, like every other industry, have had to adapt their approach over time, moving away from first generic organic post, then into image- and video-based advertising to make use of the tools that were given to us.

Like organic social content, paid social content has followed a similar path, with a video first approach. Paid content is very similar to traditional posts from travel brands, albeit usually with a more offer or promotional approach. For paid social posts to cut through with both users but also the algorithms, the creative skills either internally or through agencies have had to be increasingly leaned on as time has gone on, as Meta and others have prioritized fresh and 'interesting' content from advertisers over other elements like production values. There was a point a few years ago when the algorithms were still primitive, and when a campaign was live for a week or so performance would start to drop, purely due to the length of time it had been live. A hack was to copy the adset in Meta, give it a new name, and then republish, and voila! Performance would come back strong within a day or two.

These days, things are a bit more sophisticated as the Meta and TikTok algorithms have billions of data points from billions of users over many years. The networks now know that entertaining, educational and interesting content is what keeps users scrolling and so reward advertisers that can deliver this style of content increasingly. For travel brands, this has meant several changes to how paid content is created and then posted out over time.

Of all the areas of digital that are discussed in this chapter, this one is the one that probably changed the most and will most likely continue to. My own experience with paid social is not what it is with all the other channels and, more importantly, whatever ideas might be noted as of today, might well be different in 12 months' time. If you are going to invest in a big paid social campaign, then it's worth noting that the puck moves quite a lot based off what the platforms see as trends in user behaviour and then asking advertisers to follow a similar direction.

But there are still some fundamentals that I will highlight here that can help you to review the output of your team, your agency or even your own efforts to improve things:

- **Be authentic:** Of course we need be authentic with our social media content – this has been the mantra since day one. But I mean genuinely authentic. Show the people who make your travel happen. Show stories from guests about how they felt. Show the locations and routes in all of their glory. If we can show our brands as real as the journeys that people will go on, we will have a much higher success both in terms of the ads cut through but also the emotion generated from users interacting with them. And please, if you have to use AI, do so for editing or touching up assets rather than creating them.

- **Use different campaign types:** Travel is big business on social and companies like Meta want to capitalize on this to get more pounds and dollars. In the last few years, specific ad campaign types have been created and rolled out to help us sell more. Meta has rolled out travel ads, flight ads and even destination ads as campaign types to help you promote specific parts of your product catalogue. New campaign types and features will undoubtedly be added to as time goes on, all of which are designed to help travel brands specifically. It is worth testing these out as, while they are designed for travel, it doesn't necessarily mean that they will deliver the best results for you as more traditional types could work better.

- **Keep iterating:** If there is anything we know about social, it's that things change over time. What worked a few years ago in terms of content and approach probably won't work now. And to make things even more challenging, content that is a few weeks old can sometimes lose its impact. Users do not want to see the same things when they scroll and if they do, are unlikely to take much action on the sixth time of seeing something. Whatever you do with your paid social ads, keep testing new ideas, messaging, length, orientation, content and style as much as you can while keeping things on brand. To stay ahead, you will need to adapt your approach to find the small wins that are available rather than hunting for big ones.

- **Link your data:** One of the biggest challenges of social is that the platforms want to keep their users on their platforms to do whatever tasks they need. They know that when users click off, they don't often come back, which isn't good for business. So, if they do, then the social networks need to know what happens. The Meta pixel is a piece of tracking code that can watch visitors from Facebook or Instagram on your website and see what happens. When set up correctly, this can be hugely valuable to not only prove success of your campaigns, but also help Meta to optimize to future success. We'll talk about tracking and measurement in Chapter 5, but for now be aware that tracking on social, where direct action is less than search or email, is perhaps more important to help you understand the value of your paid media.

Email marketing

While social media has been the darling of the marketing press for the last decade, it doesn't mean it is the only way to sell your travel products. Email marketing has been around for decades but is still a large part our of digital marketing toolbox. Email is still one of the most common activities when going online and for anyone doing a desk job, it usually forms a large part of our working day. For many, email is an 'old' tactic and 'dying' but the numbers don't really seem to play that out. Research carried out by

SparkToro in 2024 outlines that open and click-through rates on emails over the last two decades has barely budged at around 25 per cent open rate on average and click-through rates of about 2 per cent (Figure 3.2).[14] Each brand will vary around these numbers, but this is the general average I've seen over my years reviewing email accounts, too.

Why does email continue to perform so well over such a long time? There are number of reasons, but the biggest one is the simple fact that email is there as a utility. Email is a simple way to send a message from one person to another or, in our case, from our business to many people at once. And, generally, we like getting things sent to us to open and read through. Of course, marketers being marketers, we've overdone it in the past and 'spammed' people too much, which has turned them off from our own marketing as well as tarnished the reputation of email in general.

But for anything important in our lives, mortgages, household bills, professional and personal documentation, our world is built with email still very much central to it. Therefore, regardless of if you are 18 or 88, chances are you will have an email account and look at it regularly. The other big thing to note is that, largely, how email is sent and received hasn't really changed over time. Social networks struggle to balance making content relevant and discovery against keeping users on their platforms as long as possible to show them more ads and make money. Email doesn't have this problem. When emails are sent, the brand sending them is charged, and on an individual basis level there is no cost.

Most importantly, perhaps, is that the relationship is still directly one-to-one – a travel brand sending directly to one recipient with no middleman controlling if the message lands or is ordered below/above someone else, as we have with social. And if the recipient wants to, they can respond back directly too. Additionally, there is no public arena to change our behaviour. This is unique to email, with perhaps the exception of text messaging, where communications happen without too much interference from a billion-dollar company trying to monetize our efforts for their own ends.

As a travel brand, you should utilize email to reach back to existing travellers to get them to find out about more of your products, offers and other inspirational content that you have to offer them. It should be seen primarily as a retention channel and should be thought about in that context. Unless you partner with someone else or have an incredible email newsletter sign-up offer or policy, you're not going to grow your email list hugely with anything other than existing travellers who opt in to receive your marketing communications when they book with you.

FIGURE 3.2 Email open and click-through rates (2005–24)

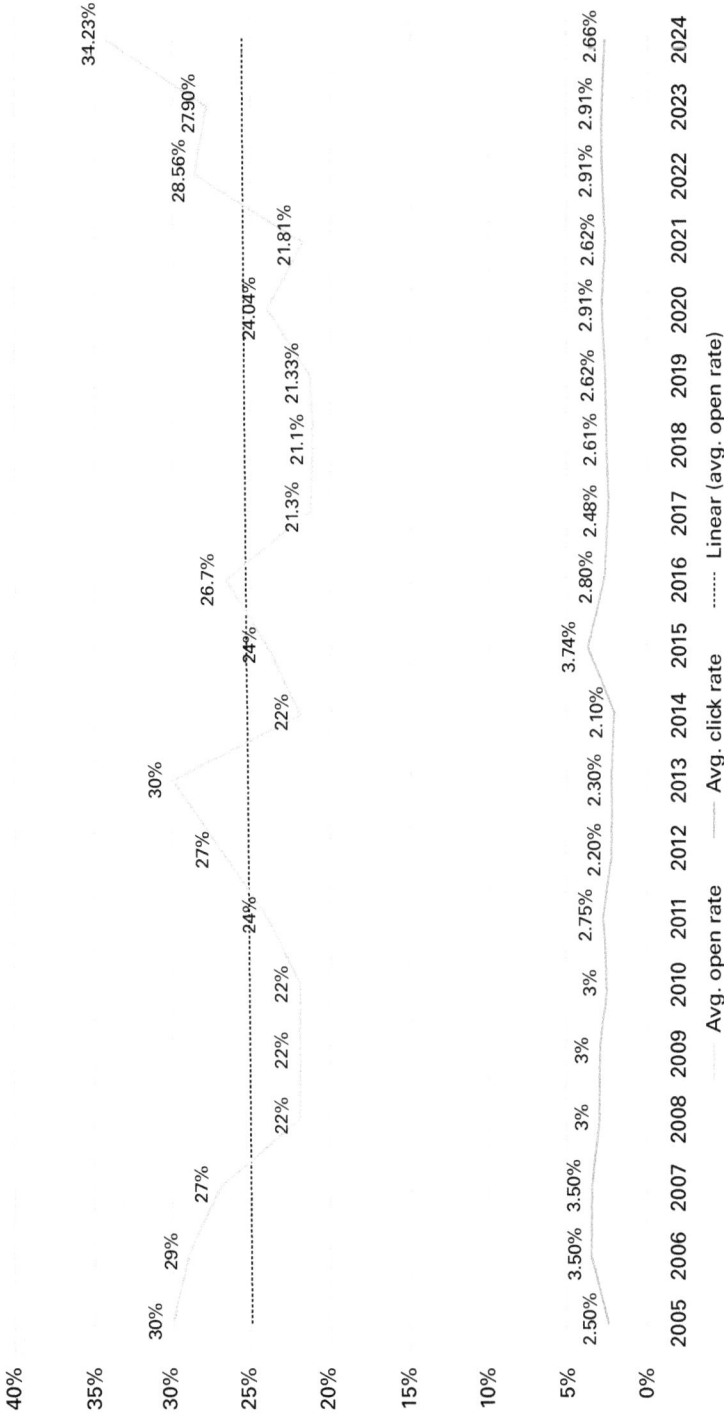

SOURCE Courtesy of Rand Fishkin, Sparktoro (2024)

But with this also comes a certain value. The people on your list *should* have had a positive experience with your business. They should've enjoyed the trip that they went on and the great memories that you created with them. Therefore, they should be open to reading more from you and being inspired again to book in the future. Unlike social media, there is no algorithm in the way of you and your previous traveller. It's within your control to own that communication channel without interference and make the most of it.

If you are looking to do better with your email marketing, here are some quick tips for you to put into practice:

- **Design for mobile first:** Like web browsing, email marketing to travellers is largely mobile first. Whatever you send out should be tested in a mobile view first, rather than desktop. This will vary depending on the demographic of your audience, but even if you are heavy on desktop still, all the trends tend to support ongoing growth on mobile devices. Even back in 2018, open rates on mobile for the travel category were at 55.6 per cent![15]

- **Test, test and test again!** While we've had email marketing tools for years now, it still stuns me how poor some of the templates and code are that come from the big email platforms. If you're doing any sort of ongoing email communication, it's important to test how your emails will show up in people inboxes to make sure that they look their best when they are opened. The biggest devices to focus on are still Apple iPhone, Gmail (web and mobile app) and Outlook (web and mobile app).

- **Split and segment:** Your email list will evolve over time in terms of the data you collect and the people on it. People will change email addresses, move home, leave the country, pass away, have changes in circumstances and many other life events. The things that they were interested in might not be what they want now. If you have groups of users who are actively opening and clicking on your emails and groups who haven't opened your last 50 emails, then you should be treating them differently! Automating your segments can be a real-time saver.

- **Don't be afraid to cull!** The days of 'big is best' are on the wane. Just because your email list has 100,000 people on it, it doesn't mean that it's any good. If you've spammed your own database over the years and they no longer open your emails or take action, then what's the point of having such a big list? And if you've emailed the same person for a year after an initial enquiry and they've taken no action, is it worth keeping them on your list? While emails are cheap to send, that doesn't mean you can keep on growing your list endlessly. Having an annual review of your recipients and seeing who is active, not interested and anything in-between can help keep your lists in the best shape, as well as helping with your General Data Protection Regulation (GDPR) obligations.

Display marketing

To complete this section of the biggest areas of digital marketing, let's look quickly at display marketing. As mentioned in Chapter 1, display marketing was the origin of digital marketing in the mid-1990s. And it's still here in the 2020s too, albeit in a totally different landscape. The display marketing world is largely owned by the two big platforms from Google and Meta, both of which give the opportunity for us to put visual banners and videos of different shapes and sizes in front of potential travellers based on certain criteria we can set.

Display marketing is probably last on the list of channels you should spend your time and money on. In my experience working across all digital marketing campaigns, it is rare for any campaign to have much direct benefit from spending on display marketing. Obviously, the purpose of display is completely different to, say, search marketing through PPC; display is there to remind travellers of your brand, versus search where the traveller is actively looking for something specific. But comparing the two against each other isn't fair as they are different beasts. With that said, it's rare that any spend on Google Display Network has added anything obviously beneficial to our clients' campaigns, and my recommendation to you is to only spend money on it if you have extra budget available (in which case, lucky you!) or you have some extra offers to promote that are worth of trying to get in front of the right audiences.

The Google Display Network (GDN) is notorious for having low-quality inventory within it and therefore the opportunity for you to align yourself to the right places for your brand is usually limited. As illustrated with our friend Ed Sheeran in Chapter 2, we need to think long and hard about our brand and the placements that we make with it. If you're selling holidays or trips of any value, you wouldn't really want to associate with a free throw-away game downloaded on the Play Store aimed at under 12s. Yes, there are settings and set-ups that you can implement to mitigate showing in irrelevant places, but with Google Ads' Performance Max (PMax) campaigns currently being difficult to control, your ads, particularly in a PMax world, will end up in display. My advice is to try to put controls in place to stop you putting ads in display as best you can.

Otherwise, if you must spend on display advertising or want to try it out, remember that nearly all users will have some element of 'banner blindness', meaning they will just detune or not 'see' them while being online or at least have any recall of them. But let's say you do want to give it a try. If it is at all possible within your brand guidelines or creative team, your best bet is to go as big and bold as you possibly can. If no one is going to really 'see' or click on your ads, then what have you got to lose? Creating ads and images that stand out in some way must be your number one priority, otherwise you're going to be costly digital wallpaper in much the same way as your competitors are. There isn't much more to add to this small section, as my belief is that, for you reading this, display is probably not where you should be spending your budget.

Setting a digital marketing budget

We've now looked at all the major channels that travel companies typically spend their digital marketing budgets on. There are always going to be new types of campaigns that can be set up within these platforms and perhaps even new platforms that crop up in the next decade (who would've thought TikTok would get so big back in the late 2010s when it first arrived?) that you should keep an eye on. For now, though, I would expect the main bulk of your budget to stay similar year on year, albeit with costs increasing across the board as time goes on.

When you spend your digital marketing budget on generating leads for your travel business, then what percentages are 'good' for each channel and what is a 'typical' set-up? I have to level with you here and say that there is no standard answer to this.

Every travel company, every budget, every target audience will always be unique. As marketers and as humans, we crave as much certainty as we can get to make sure we don't get things wrong. We'd much rather not be wrong than get things wildly right and so want to see what others are doing and check how far away we are from them. It's part of the reason I think that social media took over in the 2010s when some companies started investing time and energy into it and saw some success, which led others to follow suit because they assumed that the other companies knew what they were doing.

Even now, we see reports showing supposed spend of competitors to our travel clients which demonstrate they spend X per cent more per month on certain phrases or channels. However, we have no idea whether the activity that a competitor undertakes makes any profit for them or not. Waste is prevalent across the industry, so just because your competitor spends a lot on Meta ads, it doesn't mean it's working for them! A potential client I spoke to spent $40,000 in two months on Google Ads. If I was their competitor, I'd perhaps think 'Hang on, they must know something I don't, they are spending big – let's try to compete against them!' It turned out that for that spend they were only able to directly attribute a single $12,000 booking. Not the best ROI, I'm sure you will agree.

To start with a budget plan, or perhaps a budget review, we need to refer back to Chapter 2 and think about our business goals. Are we trying to grow rapidly in the long term and sell? Are we trying to build a sustainable business with smaller targets and get to a less risky cash balance for the shareholders? Are we looking to expand into new markets or get more from our existing ones? Have the audiences and places you work with changed dramatically due to macro events? There will be many things to consider in terms of what the next 12 to 36 months could look like for your company, but having a plan can at least help to set a course for direction.

I won't hide behind an 'it depends' answer and leave it at that. Let's try to illustrate how a typical budget for a travel business turning over £10 million a year in sales might look. Table 3.6 is a typical split of budget spend in terms of direct cost (not including staff or agency fees) against what Google Analytics might report from one of its traffic conversion reports.

TABLE 3.6 Example breakdown of how budget might be split and how sales might be measured in Google Analytics

Channel	Budget %	Sales %	Notes
Organic search (brand)	0%	25%	This should be users just typing in your brand name and finding your company, and as such there is no real cost to be attributed.
Organic search (non brand)	25%	10%	Putting effort into SEO to get ranked for relevant generic phrases takes time and investment but should generate a noticeable percentage of your sales.
Paid search (brand)	5%	25%	Ideally you shouldn't spend at all on brand traffic, but if you have to then keep it to a minimum, otherwise it'll take away your organic clicks and make you pay for things you'd have got anyway!

(continued)

TABLE 3.6 (Continued)

Channel	Budget %	Sales %	Notes
Paid search (non brand)	50%	20%	Going non-brand is expensive, and cost per leads/booking can be in the hundreds. Check your reports and attribution in depth to understand where the best spend is being achieved and do more of that!
Organic social media	0–5%	0–5%	Your spend here might include internal costs or freelancers (or your own time!). Typically, most travel businesses see little to no return on their organic posts, so set your expectations low for a directly attributable return.
Paid social media	5–10%	0–5%	Again, seeing a direct return from any paid ads that you might run is often hard unless you have specific deals that are only available through social channels.
Email marketing	0–5%	10–20%	Depending on how good your lists and offers are, this will give varying degrees of success, but if done right it can be one of the most profitable channels you have to get bookings from repeat travellers.
Display advertising	0–5%	0–5%	As discussed earlier, display is a branding channel and not likely to show up much in terms of your sales reports or attribution, and other channels are likely to be a better bet.

As to how much a £10 million company might spend on marketing overall, again, this will depend on how aggressive someone might want to grow or be in their part of the travel sector overall. For an independently owned travel business of that size, though, it is typically between 5 and 8 per cent of overall revenue in total.

As outlined earlier, these are by no means set numbers. How much you have available and your own objectives will dictate how much is spent on what and when. It may also seem a little nonsensical to spend so much budget on non-search channels when they deliver so little in terms of per cent of overall sales. Search marketing though is an acquisition channel rather than a brand one. We should be using search to attract new customers predominantly so that we can then sell back to them in the future through email, social and ideally organic brand searches. If we do not keep acquiring new travellers through search (or anything else, for that matter), then in the end all the other channels will start to drop in numbers over time too.

It is crucial to always remember that search is only ever harvesting the traffic that is already happening for certain destinations or trip types. The channel itself is not going to increase the number of searches made or the new places that people might go. That is achieved through social media and a variety of offline tactics which we'll look at in the next chapter. If you're looking to grow your travel brand, it's very important to have an idea of the current share of the search market you have within some of the phrases/areas you're already doing well in and want to grow more of.

If you're at, say, 70 per cent of the available search demand already, but want to grow overall sales by 150 per cent in the next three years, then you have a big challenge. If there is only 30 per cent more that you can get in search (and typically the more search share you get on Google, the more you end up paying for that last 10–20 per cent of the market) you're going to have to find new channels, routes to market or products that you can sell.

To hit your 150 per cent target, your budget splits and focus would need to look quite different to Table 3.6, with perhaps a much bigger focus on both organic and paid social to raise awareness of your brand and products in your audience. You might then have to find ways of capturing email addresses or other data to then sell to new travellers through more of your owned channels, rather than keep on spending on premium spaces.

Summary

Ultimately, there is no right or wrong answer as to what your budget should be or how it should split. With that said, there are some answers which are more right than wrong! From my experience, there is sadly a widespread reliance on Google Ads for generating leads and bookings. Some companies spend up to 80 per cent of their marketing budget on Google Ads each year. They have become almost addicted to their Google Ads accounts and the ROI that it can bring.

While this has worked in the past and still might do as you read this, being so reliant on one channel for your travel business to thrive is an incredibly dangerous position to be in. Spreading your marketing across more channels might bring more complexity and cost, but in the long run will build a better and stronger marketing approach that delivers better results over a longer period. If you are going to review your marketing budgets and approach because of this book, then please do make sure you spread your marketing around and don't put all your clicks into one basket!

In this chapter I've looked at the different marketing channels that are available to modern marketers, why you'd potentially use them and the pros and cons of each. It's worth bearing in mind that what is right for one travel business in terms of budget and focus split might not be right for the other, which I've highlighted here. But becoming reliant on one or several digital channels poses a risk and over time you should consider using some offline marketing techniques to widen your reach. There is so much that digital marketing can offer when it comes to offline, which we'll look at more closely in the next chapter.

Notes

1 A Nirgudka. Porter, M. E. 1996. What is a strategy? *Harvard Business Review* (November–December): 61–78. Management and Accounting Web, 2002. maaw.info/ArticleSummaries/ArtSumPorter96.htm (archived at https://perma.cc/ NJS9-5NV7)

2 Ivy Exec. Most CMOs don't last, here's how to beat the trend, Ivy Exec, 2021. ivyexec.com/career-advice/2021/cmo-tenures/ (archived at https://perma. cc/9NDR-SCAK)

3 Marketing Week. CMOs have the shortest tenure in the C-suite, Marketing Week, 2024. www.marketingweek.com/cmos-shortest-tenure-c-suite/ (archived at https://perma.cc/MA37-PJ63)

4 D Goodwin. Google Now sees more than 5 billion searches per year, Search Engine Land, 2025. searchengineland.com/google-5-trillion-searches-per-year-452928 (archived at https://perma.cc/E6LS-VYNG)

5 T B Lee. Google's big break: How Bill Gross's GoTo.com inspired the AdWords business model, Slate, 2013. slate.com/business/2013/10/googles-big-break-how-bill-gross-goto-com-inspired-the-adwords-business-model.html (archived at https://perma.cc/K293-7KYV)

6 Statista. Media influences on travel destination, Statista, nd. www.statista.com/ chart/30135/media-influences-on-travel-destination/ (archived at https://perma. cc/79GE-S6TS)

7 I El Qudsi. Are the days of organic social media reach over? Forbes, 2023. www.forbes.com/councils/forbesagencycouncil/2023/04/27/are-the-days-of-organic-social-media-reach-over/ (archived at https://perma.cc/ZV82-CJF4)

8 We Are Social. Digital 2025, We Are Social, 2025. wearesocial.com/uk/blog/2025/02/digital-2025/ (archived at https://perma.cc/SUY2-YMZ6)

9 Meltwater. The state of social media 2024: Thank you, Meltwater, nd. www.meltwater.com/en/state-of-social-media-thank-you (archived at https://perma.cc/H2YC-4VZB)

10 We Are Social. Digital 2025, We Are Social, 2025. wearesocial.com/uk/blog/2025/02/digital-2025/ (archived at https://perma.cc/DMX7-7NMF)

11 Meta Platforms, Inc. Meta's opening statement slides, Meta, 2023. s3.documentcloud.org/documents/25896886/metas-opening-statement-slides.pdf (archived at https://perma.cc/T2HU-RS5M)

12 ABTA. Holiday Habits 2024–25, ABTA, 2024. www.abta.com/industry-zone/reports-and-publications/abta-holiday-habits-reports/holiday-habits-2024-25 (archived at https://perma.cc/BZY2-8FJL)

13 We Are Social. Digital 2025, We Are Social, 2025. wearesocial.com/uk/blog/2025/02/digital-2025/ (archived at https://perma.cc/HR9K-GAVK)

14 R Fishkin. Email is the most consistent, reliable marketing channel on the web (and I can prove it), SparkToro, 2024. sparktoro.com/blog/email-is-the-most-consistent-reliable-marketing-channel-on-the-web-and-i-can-prove-it/ (archived at https://perma.cc/J3HS-8VTG)

15 Email Monday. Mobile email usage statistics 2024, 2024. www.emailmonday.com/mobile-email-usage-statistics/ (archived at https://perma.cc/8JZU-W3S5)

4

Where digital and offline fit together

Introduction

Let's get this out there up front. This is a book about digital marketing. And this section talks about offline marketing. While digital marketing has been the dominate force since the turn of the century, it doesn't operate in isolation. When I first started in my career, I was fairly naïve to this fact. I'd spent a lot of time in front of a computer growing up and at university. Desktops were becoming more common in households. Then we saw broadband introduced, followed by early mobile phones with 3G, then 4G and before we could take stock, half of the world had an iPhone. The 2000s saw tremendous leaps in technology and at times it seemed constant and felt it was all that got talked about. Print? Radio? C'mon, this is the new era!

This trend carried on into the 2010s when Web 2.0 landed and we entered a new world of connectivity and connectedness, with our mobile phones never more than an arm's length away. We became glued to our screens. Then the 2020s came and the Covid-19 pandemic put the world into lockdown and pushed us even further into our screens, making it the new normal of chatting with friends, family and work colleagues anywhere in the world through our digital devices.

Recent generations have grown up only knowing screens in their lives to do almost all of their activities, living their lives in it and with it. I became all too blinkered by this. When the credit crunch happened in 2009, dozens of clients came to us each month wanting to move their marketing away from paper-based marketing to digital as it was the new thing and seen as cheaper and more controllable. To go from marketing that was done once a year, cost thousands and was untraceable, to something that could be changed at any point, with budgets that could be flexed and have clear reporting was revolutionary. Now it's just the norm.

As things become standard, and time goes on, these are just the ways of doing business. It shouldn't really be called digital marketing, it's just marketing. We made the distinction in the early days because it was new and needed a new label. In fact, the term 'digital marketing' had several different terms in the early days which evolved as the markets did. The term 'new media' was very common in the early 2000s but was dropped by the industry as it had links to physical digital media like CDs and DVDs which was also linked to the 'dot-com' bubble, a term that was something start-ups didn't want to associate with. Investors needed to buy into something new and so the term 'digital marketing' become de facto.

The digital world doesn't operate in isolation, though. We go online to be inspired about travel experiences, new places to go, food to taste, places to visit... these are real-world experiences that can't currently translate to digital. Often when we search for our next place to go, we do so because we have seen or heard something. This could be an advert on a bus shelter, an article in a magazine or a conversation with a friend.

Over time I've come to realize that the digital world, while important, isn't the only thing that motivates or influences our travellers. And for some travel audiences it has much less influence than in others. The stereotype of older age groups wanting physical marketing assets over digital is still largely true from the research that is carried out each year. But even younger audiences like to have a tangible 'thing' to flick through or share with friends, just to a lesser extent. Humans have evolved to use all senses, and a nicely produced brochure is a tangible thing that can bring your travel experiences to life in physical form. It also gives your potential travellers the chance to signal to their friends that they are about to go to somewhere nice when their friends and family pop over.

While we might *want* to reach all our potential travellers through digital means, that doesn't mean that they want to research and buy like this. We must be led by our customers and plan our marketing accordingly.

Remember – audience first

There is no point in being a marketer in any job unless you understand and follow the needs of your audience. Unless you are either lucky or are in the demographic of travellers you want to target, chances are you are going to need to do some work.

We have already talked about the importance of doing your customer research to find out more about your target traveller groups. It might be that over time there is limited change in terms of income or demographics of your audience, in which case your job might be easier than a travel business that wants to target anyone from 20 to 80 years old, where needs and behaviours could evolve within a few years.

How do different demographics respond to different media when they are looking to travel? I've already touched on the idea that stereotypes are prevalent in the media landscape – older travellers read newspapers and younger people do everything on their phones. Is this true? Well, yes and no.

Research carried out by ABTA in the UK in 2024 shows that is only partly true. From a survey of over 2,000 respondents from across the UK, nearly every generation uses general search engines (49 per cent) as well as asking their friends and family to find out where is best for the next adventure.[1] However, there is a reasonably clear divide between what I'll call younger and older travellers. For anyone under the age of 34, social media and video websites (let's assume YouTube and TikTok predominantly) are the go-to for finding inspiration. Having grown up in a mobile, digital world it's perhaps no surprise to see them score so highly.

If you think about your own travel business, which age group would you think your ideal target travellers are going to be in? Does your focus and marketing mix represent this? Should you consider running newspaper adverts again if you are targeting over 55-year-old travellers predominantly? Or if you want to target younger age groups, is podcasting on your list of marketing channels to try?

If you are in charge of your overall marketing and have a team of internal people to support you, it is worth finding and reading marketing and customer research (like the ABTA piece) to ensure you have the right skills in-house to deliver the breadth of media you need and supplement it with agency or freelancer support as required.

What is offline anyway?

The definitions of media channels we use in the 2020s have largely become symbiotic rather than meaningful. 'Digital marketing' seems to largely refer to search marketing, sometimes social media and other supporting channels in a round about way. In recent time it has seemed that 'social media marketing' is increasingly seen in its own group and treated as such, meaning two terms are largely prevalent. It's all open to interpretation depending on where your own focus is.

For now, at least, there still seems to be some clarity of what 'offline' or 'traditional' marketing means. Offline is all the things that we did pre internet era – TV, radio, newspaper ads, billboard, direct mails… the list goes on. Despite those channels being seen as traditional media, these days they are anything but. If you've ever been on the tube in London, you will see largely digital display boards when you travel down the escalators. Drive around any town and media will be animated and generated by LEDs.

That brochure you requested from the website? It was printed on a digital press and could've even been tailored to the destinations you like, using data of what you looked at prior to it being printed, pulled from your website, CRM and who knows, supported by AI plug-ins. And radio? Is radio something we turn on in the kitchen or do podcasts count as a new type of radio? Isn't radio just something broadcasted without pictures? It's a very blurry line between the two although we still think of them as completely different things, with the only real difference being when we listen to things (live or in our own time) and who creates the content.

The impact of digital technology across the board for any offline media company has been and continues to be dramatic. Whenever I hear about what is supposedly possible through older media companies, it becomes apparent that they haven't stood still in recent times. They are aware of the need for these types of media to keep up with the big digital platforms and a lot of them have invested in technology to give a much wider array of options to larger travel companies.

The focus on data behind the scenes means that even smaller travel businesses can start to engage and use their own CRM data alongside data providers who have massive data sets, to get better targeting and thus produce cost per lead measures that are often comparable to what the digital players can offer. The difficulty, though, is that most marketers have tended to stay away from 'traditional' media as it's often a longer process, outside of a skillset and perhaps not seen as 'cool' enough when presented to a boss. There may be some generalization here; however, I believe this to be representative of a lot of what I've seen.

My question to you is whether you have challenged your thinking in recent times to look beyond digital. We all want to improve our digital marketing and, search marketing, websites, newsletters and social media pretty much dominate across all age bands. But with that comes competition. And lots of it. If everyone is doing the same thing, trying to reach the same people, how will you make your brand stand out?

What if you could do a trial and put an advert in a magazine that your audience read? What if you sent them a postcard in the post to say that you miss them and want them to book again next year? How many other travel companies are doing that right now? Going offline might actually be a progressive move and one to think about.

What is the value of offline marketing?

When I first started doing my presentations to business owners in the 2000s about SEO and PPC, I would often ask the room to do a show of hands. 'How many of you click on the paid adverts at the top of the Google search results?' In a room of 50 people, I might occasionally get one hand. 'I do it to click on my competitors' ads and waste their budget!' would sometimes be the response I'd get, to much sniggering. I would then have to explain that clicking ads is a good thing for their competitors as click-through rate is part of what makes ads good, so more clicks equals improved rank and is not as detrimental to your competitors as people thought it was, but that's another point.

Whether people do or don't click on ads is somewhat moot. Customers are smart. They don't ever want to be 'sold to'. They want to find the best answers to their needs and don't want to be duped into buying something that is meeting someone else's agenda, not their own. They also don't want to be bombarded by ads all day. In fact, let's be honest, we don't want to see any ads at all really.

There are some marketing statistics, or rather shared numbers, that have gone viral over time that suggest we see anything from 3,000 to 10,000 ads per day. Like a lot of 'known marketing stats', this is total rubbish. Those levels of numbers just don't stack up at all. By simple maths of someone being awake 16 hours per day, you'd have to be seeing dozens of ads per minute. The reality is probably closer to one researcher who did a very crude measure for The Drum marketing magazine in 2023 of perhaps 100 a day.[2]

Our digital lives are fast moving and across multiple channels a lot of the time. While some younger groups spend hours a day on social media, they are not consuming or paying attention to all of the adverts that fly past their screen each minute. Yes, they are 'shown', but are they given any sort of attention at all? Typically, a lot of display campaigns run through either Google or Meta get next to no clicks or recall with travellers at all. That's not to say they don't work, it's that they are cheap media and very easily ignored.

Studies into the value of offline media against online media are out there but the one that has stuck with me the most is one from JICMail in the UK, which looked at the time spent looking at mail in 1,000 homes over a year against other media types.[3] It is a robust and long study, albeit carried out at the end of 2022 towards the end of Covid when time at home was perhaps slightly skewed compared to where we are today. But with that said, the results in terms of cost per minute with media (i.e. how long we spend looking at, say, a direct mail piece against a TV or social media advert) show that a lot of traditional media performs very well compared to digital (Figure 4.1).

Perhaps unsurprisingly, social media ads don't fare well, given how easy it is for someone to scroll past an image or video in literally a matter of seconds. Desktop display also doesn't fair great, given how 'banner blind' we have become over the last few decades. In the 1990s, getting a click-through rate of 5 per cent was sometimes achievable, but in the 2020s getting a CTR of anything above 0.1 per cent is a minor miracle.[4] Clicks and

FIGURE 4.1 Time spent with media: cost per minute with ABC1 adults in the UK

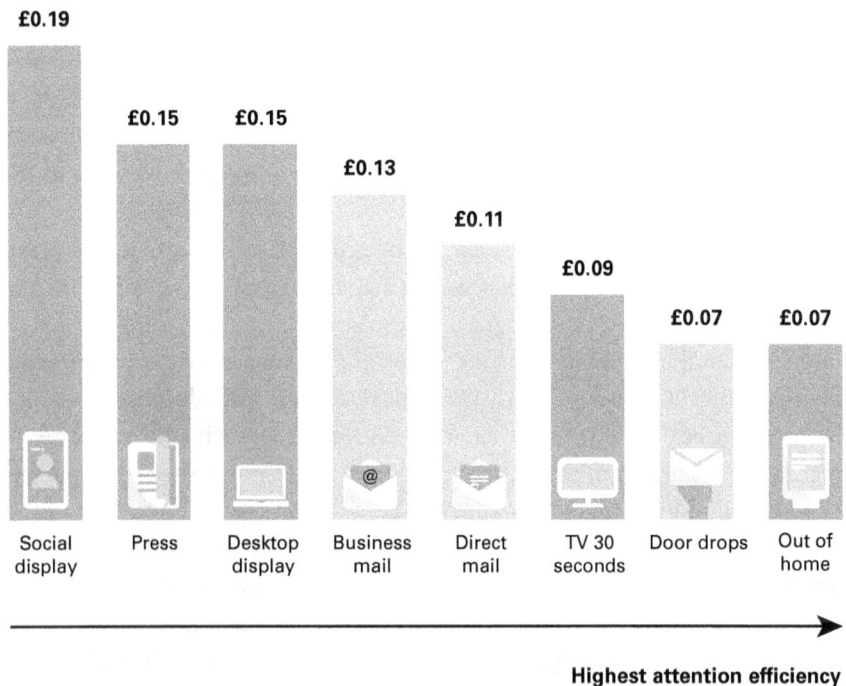

Highest attention efficiency

SOURCE Courtesy of JICMail (2022)

interactions are central to digital media, in the main. It is important to note that not all media are equal in terms of the attention that we give to them, and just because offline is 'expensive' and online is 'cheap' this isn't a great comparison in terms of value, as shown in Figure 4.1. Our job as marketers is to find the best ways to get our message to our target customers, and we must be open to different approaches to deliver the best value. A simple exercise you can put into practice around this is to combine your online data with offline media to get the best results and help achieve your objectives.

Brochures and direct mail

With the advent of digital media becoming the standard in our marketing communications, things have been tough for any direct mail business in the last few decades. Since the turn of the century, the amount of money spent has trended downward in every Western country as marketers switch their resources and budgets towards digital media. The growth of spend with Google, Meta and its counterparts has had to come from somewhere, and most offline channels have been hit with lower numbers and less attention from a marketing community standpoint.

In the US, there has been an almost halving of mail sent since 2006, down from 232 billion items sent, to 112 billion in 2024.[5] In the UK, it's a similar story with nearly £2 billion being spent on direct mail advertising in 2015,[6] dropping to around £1 billion in 2023, showing a 50 per cent decrease in less than a decade.[7] Like all non-digital media, direct mail has had to work very hard to be seen as relevant, particularly in a marketing industry which has always over emphasized the importance of younger audiences and new trends to jump on.

While not as fashionable as it once was, direct mail can still be a crucial part of the travel marketing toolbox. A holiday is an emotional purchase, made over many weeks and months, and often involving several people. For these types of purchases, having something physical on your bedside table, kitchen worktop or wherever else things get left in your house can be really important. As shown earlier, the time spent with media is something that can often get overlooked. Just because a good chunk of the things we receive in the post are of little to no value, a well-produced holiday brochure or promotional flyer can stay around for a very long time, get looked at dozens of times and help guide the traveller to their next booking.

Direct mail can be linked directly into your digital marketing plans in several ways:

- Website data on the pages viewed by known individuals can be stored in a CRM or email marketing platform if configured properly. If you are capturing website visits and are able to link them to a particular customer then over time you will be able to build a profile of the person that you have first party data on. If you sell holidays to different parts of the world or perhaps with different product options, then this data can be valuable and potentially save you money by only sending the relevant information to the relevant person, as well as potentially increasing your chances of conversion. Some direct mail companies can work with you to get API access to your systems or downloads of customer data at specific points in the year, to ensure that you get the most from your send outs.

- If you have automation journeys, then a direct link via API could help to build more touchpoints into how you interact with your customers. For certain audiences, it's worth thinking how you could potentially use direct mail to 'nudge' them through their consideration journey. If you have set up an automation workflow over say four weeks with both email and text messages but aren't getting quite the conversion rate that you want, perhaps a letter or postcard or some other physical media might be the tool to tweak your numbers up.

- Finally, if you know that you've sent a large generic mailshot to your database of customers, perhaps prior to the peak booking period (in the UK just after Christmas until roughly the end of quarter one) then after a few months you should be able to see in your CRM or booking system which customers did book and which didn't. This is useful information to then start to build out digital campaigns around, to target those travellers who received your mail but still didn't book with you. This can help inform retargeting or email campaigns, to push messages or perhaps even offers to users who may have received direct mail, visited your website off the back of it, but then didn't quite get over the line.

With any activity, it's worth trying to understand the behaviours of your audience as best as you can and then finding ways to use that data to refine and improve more. Sometimes there is an assumption that anything to do with print isn't trackable or isn't 'digital' and so should sit with another team or department in your business. I wholeheartedly believe that this is old thinking and your job as a digital travel marketer is to look at the activity happening as best you can through a data lens, and find out more information about your audience to improve any activity in the future.

TV and connected TVs

I probably don't need to tell you how much TV watching has changed with the advent of broadband internet. When getting a few megabytes a second became the norm, pretty much everything changed for TV. No longer did we have to wait until 8pm on a Thursday night to watch our favourite programme while sat on our sofa. We could watch whatever we wanted, whenever we wanted. Linear (or broadcast) TV as we know it has been on a decline along a similar, if less pronounced, trend as direct mail. In the US, less than 50 per cent of all TV watchers could be reached with linear programming in 2023, while in the UK it was considerably higher at around 79 per cent, albeit down from 83 per cent in 2022.[8]

For traditional TV channels in the UK, there has been a big promotion of their digital TV apps (often referred to as connected TV) to ensure that they stay relevant against the behemoths of Netflix and Amazon, which have millions of subscribers and increasingly take more and more time and attention away from the established brands. Additionally, in the UK roughly 28 per cent of all UK households pay for a Sky TV subscription to access real-time, on demand and app-based programming.[9]

As technology and demand have changed, so have the options for advertisers. The days of committing to weeks of continued messaging across the whole of a country or region are on the wane. With the ability to pinpoint homes by IP, city, region and even income and disposable income, we now have great targeting capabilities which can be utilized. TV has taken an approach to advertising, like what we've become accustomed to with the big digital platforms. If you want to branch out from your digital marketing options and go from small screen to large, then the barrier to entry isn't that big.

Through services like Sky AdSmart (others are available), you can run adverts over short periods of time, in specific regions and even into specific homes. How can we extend our digital marketing efforts into TV? Well, we can look at our CRM data to understand where our audiences are based, from exports of customers and enquirers based on postcode. We should be able to understand where we are getting our best revenue and profit from in the country to then either target those people at relevant times (let's assume again the peak booking period post-Christmas is a good time) or perhaps branch out to other cities with similar demographics, or surrounding ones where we've seen less success or bookings. Additionally, thanks to the large personal data sets that are available, there are options to target specific types of households, such as high net worth, frequent travellers or bargain hunters.

Like the PPC campaigns discussed earlier, we can set up different ad messaging to different groups to ensure our relevance stays as high as possible to increase our chances of conversion.

Linking this back to our digital marketing plans and campaigns, if TV advertising is something that you have the budget to run (campaigns can cost equivalent to other online options so are within reach) then before you go live, it's again worth looking at how you align this with your wider digital marketing efforts. If you are going to be in broadcast adverts in certain homes in the UK, can and should you supplement this with increased digital activity? Upping your spend on Google Ads, social channels and perhaps even email to those regions will give a 'halo effect' on your efforts where you will likely get bigger returns on your investments than if you were to complete multiple activities separately.

Simpson Travel are an established and prestigious UK-based travel company offering luxury villa and hotel holidays across Europe. Their typical clients are families and couples looking for exceptional holiday experiences for their precious summertime together. With a large amount of market and customer research, they know their current and target audience incredibly well and are able to pinpoint who they are and where they live.

Their Director of Marketing and Communications, Helen Grace, understands that a mix of marketing channels are needed to reach their clients. For their market particularly, offline marketing plays an important role in helping to spread the message of Simpson Travel as well as positioning it as a premium brand in the villa market. The use of radio ads, for example, has been tested several times over many years with varying degrees of success, sometimes bringing great results while other times bringing the wrong type of client, which in hindsight showed a slight disconnect between that audience and market.

'We know that even within the same audience and channel performance can vary depending on the message and time of year. We've learned how to best spend our budget over time, although it's not always easy to plan this nor pinpoint the exact return,' said Helen. For the Simpson audience, there is a clear benefit to using 'offline' media such as TV ads and print, which has been helpful to acquire new customers as well as re-engage lapsed travellers. 'We know that our audience prefers being inspired rather than being sold to, and use our marketing media in all formats to get our message across in the best way possible.' With that said, knowing exactly what impact each channel has had is hard. 'Sometimes we can pinpoint new channels' success when they are done in isolation, but it's getting increasingly hard to know. Attribution is tough to get right as some of our bookings take many months to come through. Increasingly we're going back to our ideal client profiles and linking our marketing plans to their lifestyles rather than trying too hard to measure everything. It's taking a certain leap of faith, but we're making good progress over time,' she added.

Simpson Travel is a great example of how, when used correctly, offline marketing can really deliver a direct impact on both booking and profitability. Using smart customer research and channel selection, they have shown that offline channels still have great benefits when used correctly. As time goes on, they are linking more first party (data that they own) with third party data together to not only find ways to improve their ongoing digital marketing efforts but also try new offline channels such as podcasts to try to increase both awareness and direct sales. 'With the first quarter of each year still a big time for bookings, we use certain channels like podcasts to help us in the build-up to that, with other channels taking over in our busy periods. We're looking forward to improving our modelling as time goes on to help us get even smarter with our approach and continuing our growth.'

Podcasts and radio

One of the biggest changes I've made in my own media consumption in the last decade is around podcasts. I've listened to literally thousands of hours of conversations from some of the greatest politicians, musicians, comedians and marketers sharing their secrets and insights. It was a journey (in both senses!) that I first started over a decade ago when I had enough 3G signal on my commute to listen to (not watch!) TED talks in my car via YouTube to help me expand my knowledge and listen in on conferences from around the world that I couldn't attend in person. This was in an era when podcasts had fallen out of favour, having been a 'big thing' in the mid-2000s, then seemingly getting forgotten about as video took over and the fragmented nature of how podcasts were accessed through dozens of different apps made it hard to access multiple shows easily.

While music has suffered from the consolidation of listening into a handful of global music platforms, podcasts have undoubtedly benefited from the easy access and global reach that has been offered from this new distribution channel. The landmark moment in this shift perhaps happened in 2020, when controversial podcaster Joe Rogan signed an exclusive agreement with Spotify for $100 million dollars.[10] At the time the deal was made, it made Rogan's output worth more than any musician on the platform and perhaps paved the way for other podcasts to become media brands or personalities in a similar way. Five years on from that deal and podcast listeners in the UK have risen 20 per cent to nearly 30 per cent of the UK population, thanks to even more audio content being produced each week by more and more creators.[11]

Podcasts have become popular as they are available to listen to whenever you want or need, which again is a representation of our time compared to 'old' radio which, like TV, had to be consumed when it was broadcast. Due to it being relatively easy to generate podcasts, many travel brands have created them, with varying degrees of success. Conde Nast Traveler, *The Independent* and travel franchise business Not Just Travel have launched many podcast channels and episodes, while many travel operators have created bespoke podcast series on specific locations from Italy to Switzerland to China and everything in between. If you want to find out about a city, country or type of holiday, someone out there has created a podcast on it! For any travel brand or influencer wanting to reach travellers in a different medium or in a more intimate way, podcasts are certainly a route to market that can pay off in the long term.

The impact of podcasts on traditional radio listening is noticeable both in terms of the numbers and also the devices. Established audio brands like the BBC and Global have had to invest heavily in their app ecosystem to ensure that their content can be accessed both in real-time and on demand, and in both apps and smart speakers. While smart speakers didn't deliver on some of their promise to change how we consumed search, it still has a small place in the home (usually in the kitchen) to listen to both music and podcasts while we get on with our lives. Radio is still in the 20–30 million listeners per month level across the UK (around half of all UK adults) across various radio brands. The numbers are not what they once were but unlike traditional TV, radio has held up fairly well due to the uniqueness of the media, which can be consumed almost anywhere and anytime.

As digital marketers, if budget and resources dictate, then advertising through podcasts should be something to consider. As with the changes in options around TV advertising, we have similar options with our audio marketing choices, too. Adverts can be targeted regionally, at specific audiences and placed around supporting content. For example, you could choose to feature in specific lifestyle shows, or travel related shows, or perhaps if you know your audience have a particular interest, let's say food or finance, there will be an option to place a 30–60 second ad spot in that show.

As well as thinking about advertising options, if you or your brand have specific expertise and credibility around a niche, then you should also think about any potential PR opportunities that might be relevant where you or someone from your brand can be a guest speaker. This could be anything from a daily consumer-related show on the BBC through to a small, niche podcaster creating something in their spare time. People are listening to audio in so many places, and as a marketer it's worth remembering this to try to find opportunities to promote your travel brand. Is radio a digital channel? Is a podcast a digital channel? If most of the content is consumed through a phone app, then you could perhaps argue that it is, although it's never talked about in the same way as social or search. Either way, it's worth you at least knowing and considering it if you want to make your mark and increase your brand presence outside of the usual places.

Out-of-home and billboards

Finally for our offline options, we could consider large-scale advertising in the shape of 'out-of-home' adverts. These are ones which can be seen by roadsides, bus shelters, train stations and anywhere else where there is any high density or flow of people. These adverts can be attached to people's houses, put up in the middle of fields, in your face when visiting a public toilet and anywhere in between. Since the invention of the advertising bus shelter by Jean-Claude Decaux in Lyon in 1964[12] we've seen millions of adverts run across the world in all sorts of places. The success of these adverts has built many global companies. You'll see 'JC Decaux' at the bottom of a good chunk of the large out-of-home adverts when walking through any city in a lot of the Western world.

In the years since 1964, not a lot changed. Find a high traffic area where there are lots of eyeballs and then place a large, printed advert up for people to see. A person on a ladder leaning against one of these boards with a large piece of paper covered in glue, trying to push it into place with a large broom was something I'd often see on my way around town in my youth. When that paper was subjected to the elements (or teenagers) over the weeks that followed, the corners of sheets would start to peel off until the next poster went up a month or two later. This format of print, paste and repeat might've had some issues but clearly worked as JC Decaux was worth over \$3 billion in market cap in 2025.[13] Many similar companies operating in the out-of-home advertising industry have also found success, with the one of the biggest in the UK being Global, who also own a number of media brands.

Out-of-home adverts have been used by international brands to keep their company logo and message front and centre for decades. You would be hard pushed to go very far in the world without seeing a fast food, fizzy drink or global make-up brand at some point on your journey. These adverts have helped keep a lot of consumer brands top of mind as well as helping to promote any campaign activities through time. They know that, despite the huge switch towards digital in this century, out-of-home is still important.

These days, if you have enough budget, you are able to run out-of-home adverts in much the same way you can with a digital display campaign. While the number of sites of digital out-of-home (DOOH) screens compared to traditional print screens is still comparatively small, with exact figures unknown, it is growing rapidly at around 8 per cent per year.[14] The technology behind these large-scale screens and boards has grown fantastically in recent years, with data connectivity being worked on in the background by the various companies who own and run the sites. While not a 'traditional' digital channel historically, as time goes on it is getting to the point where it could be seen as a digital outlet. It is now possible to buy advertising space in specific locations around the country, at specific times of day and with specific and flexible messaging. As these screens are powered by digital creative and algorithms they could easily be compared against Meta, Google and other platforms, albeit on a much larger physical scale.

And it isn't stopping there. Technology that has been rolled out in recent years is going a step further. Some sites are now able to generate real-time adverts based specifically on the gender, income and even the faces of the people that might 'see' or interact with the signs around them. Of course, we can't change adverts on a motorway based on the people driving along them (at least not yet) but in high footfall areas like shopping centres some of these digital out-of-home advert panels contain built-in cameras and touch-screens that allow passers-by to interact.

For us as marketers, if we know that the customers that we want to target are under 30, we could perhaps know that they are more likely to go to shopping centres at weekends or after work than during the day. The ability to pick our time of day and places within a shopping centre, perhaps nearer the shops we know or would assume they are more likely to drop into, gives us great precision about who, where and when we show our adverts.

Reporting our campaigns is again as granular as we get in our other digital channels; numbers of impressions, locations around an area, perhaps even 'interactions' if we have set things up in a specific way… it is all very comparable yet not often thought about in the 'digital' context.

My opinion is that most digital marketers have grown up in a world of almost exclusively Google and Meta and therefore it's become the norm. If I use Google to search and then spend a large chunk of my day on Instagram and TikTok, then why wouldn't I just use those platforms to target my users? Of course, this makes complete sense. And for most travel brands, budgets to spend on advertising aren't great with every pound being scrutinized. I am a very big believer in concentrating budget into less, not more, channels as I've seen first-hand the dilution that happens when companies try too many things at the same time and end up achieving next to nothing. However, the features and flexibility we get from newer media like DOOH means we can start to branch out or at least test our advertising in newer places. This is why the likes of Virgin Atlantic and Sherwood Hotels along with destinations like Aruba and Los Angeles are spending on DOOH.[15]

Making it fit

As I've said many times, it does depend on your specific marketing objectives for the coming years. A lot of offline advertising media are not what we could call direct response. That is to say, if someone sees a billboard advertisement today, they are unlikely to make a purchase in the next 24 hours, and most likely not with travel.

As mentioned at the beginning of this chapter, most of the brands that you see on these media are multinational fast-moving consumer goods (FMCG) brands who keep pushing their logo and message to us. They know that repetition is the key to success. There is a good reason why Coca-Cola, McDonalds and many others continue to spend billions of pounds each year on advertising. We know who they are, we've all bought their products. Yet, if they stopped advertising then chances are we wouldn't be buying so much or so often over time.

Building and keeping that brand awareness takes time and ongoing investment. Not many companies anywhere in the world have this luxury or necessity to consistently invest in large-scale broadcast media. And I don't believe many travel brands do, outside of the largest OTAs in the world like Booking.com, Expedia and Airbnb, who have huge investment and pressure from the stock markets. They are platforms that go for scale and reach across dozens of countries globally. Most travel brands are not this and so it makes no sense to copy what they do.

A large number of travel brands, perhaps the one that you're working for now, serve maybe only a few thousand passengers a year and turn over revenue in the millions, not hundreds of millions or billions. Our marketing challenges are very different! The challenge of being noticed by our audience is big enough in these increasingly fragmented times. Getting people to click to our website, watch our videos and open our communications online is something that every travel brands wants to improve on. This is all while we aim to show that our marketing efforts are 'working' now through monthly reporting data provided to us by the likes of Google, Meta and others. We need to demonstrate as best we can that the money we've spent has delivered passengers and profit to our company. We'll go deep on this in the next section.

Having the need, budget and internal support to work in the longer term, brand-oriented channels are something that not every travel brand can afford to do. The argument to be made though is that if every travel brand is doing the same with their marketing channels, the direction of travel is only going to be one of increased cost and competition in the longer term. To build a 'brand' where you are either top of mind or at least part of a small consideration set is a very long-term and hard to measure play, and one that takes time to achieve. But if we don't take action to use some of the offline media discussed in this chapter then we're going to struggle to improve marketing results massively unless we take better action and are bolder with our communications.

The data we have in our digital systems can and should be used to help guide our online and offline marketing efforts. We have information about our travellers, sometimes going back decades, detailing what they have bought, where they have travelled, where they live in the country, how old they are and many other data points. We don't want to use this information in an inappropriate way – we want to *understand* our travellers more. If we know that certain types of people buy certain types of holidays or trips, then this should ideally be used to help us sell more to more people or help our travel business make more profit. If we know what messages resonate best in terms of generating enquiries online, then we should be able to take these themes and ideas and run them in an offline context, or vice versa.

To think of offline and online as separate entities is an outdated view of the world. With the information we can get about our offline advertising in terms of impressions, messages, placements geographically and even interaction points, we can start to treat both advertising channels in a similar way.

Summary

By taking a neutral approach to how we market ourselves, we can not only make better choices, but we can also make better comparisons around the effectiveness of our campaigns. We have to always remind ourselves that the numbers we see in terms of digital channels are only a version of the truth. Digital marketing data is only ever showing one version of the story, and a lot of the time that story is going to favour the platform that delivered the advert and spent our money. We will explore this more in the next chapter.

While an advert in a magazine might have an uncountable number of actual reads and views, it doesn't necessarily mean it is less important. One brochure sent to the right potential traveller at the right time might have a way cheaper cost per conversion than 50 emails or 10 PPC clicks. Just because digital media is shown to someone, it doesn't mean that it was truly seen, remembered or made any connection to the person.

Digital marketing is crucial and I would argue for most travel businesses it should be the main focus of activity and spend of your budget. But I do hope that this chapter has made you rethink what 'digital' is in this modern world, when nearly all offline channels have some sort of comparable measure to the digital world and can be bought in a similar way.

When all of your competitors are likely doing the same activity as you with digital advertising, it means that over time our competition is going to increase, and our costs will rise. Our job as marketers is to try to be as effective as possible with our marketing budgets. We have to place the best bets we can with our budgets and hope that they pay back both in the short and long term.

There is no guarantee of success. We can only learn from others and ourselves to make better bets. Obviously by reading this book, you are hoping to shortcut some of that! But sometimes we have to adapt our strategy to find new ways to get better returns. Putting aside some budget into offline channels and starting small with perhaps a direct mail campaign to a list of travellers who booked over two years ago but haven't travelled since, or a connected TV advertising run for a three month campaign in the best area of the country where your travellers live, could be a way into a new approach that helps you achieve your goals a little better in the next 12 months.

Notes

1   ABTA. ABTA reveals where people get their holiday inspiration, ABTA, 2025.
    www.abta.com/news/abta-reveals-where-people-get-their-holiday-inspiration
    (archived at https://perma.cc/EL3A-SRCG)

2   S Anderson. How many ads do we really see in a day? Spoiler: it's not 10,000,
    The Drum, 2023. www.thedrum.com/news/2023/05/03/how-many-ads-do-we-
    really-see-day-spoiler-it-s-not-10000 (archived at https://perma.cc/GNM3-AXXZ)

3   JICMail. Mail attention, JICMail, 2025. www.jicmail.org.uk/data/attention-
    the-time-we-spend-with-mail/ (archived at https://perma.cc/FB6A-AZFR)

4   Wikipedia. Click-through rate, Wikipedia, 2025. en.wikipedia.org/wiki/
    Click-through_rate (archived at https://perma.cc/Y9WT-EP7D)

5   Statista. United States Postal Service's total mail volume from 2004 to 2024,
    Statista, 2025. www.statista.com/statistics/320234/mail-volume-of-the-usps/
    (archived at https://perma.cc/3YR4-85MA)

6   Decision Magazine. Direct mail spend bullish at £2bn+, Decision Magazine,
    2015. www.decisionmarketing.co.uk/news/direct-mail-spend-to-stay-at-2bn
    (archived at https://perma.cc/HPM6-9VH7)

7   Statista. Direct mail advertising expenditure in the United Kingdom (UK) from
    2014 to 2023, Statista, 2024. www.statista.com/statistics/262729/direct-mail-
    advertising-revenue-in-the-uk/ (archived at https://perma.cc/YV8W-X8JR)

8   Videoweek. Advertisers are turning off linear TV quicker than viewers,
    Videoweek, 2024. videoweek.com/2024/01/17/advertisers-are-turning-off-
    linear-tv-quicker-than-viewers/ (archived at https://perma.cc/M53A-H65S)

9   Statista. Leading TV broadcasters in the United Kingdom (UK) as of October
    2024, by audience share, Statista, 2024. www.statista.com/statistics/269983/
    leading-tv-broadcasters-in-the-uk-by-audience-share/ (archived at https://
    perma.cc/M4W3-HF6P)

10 BBC. Why Joe Rogan's exclusive Spotify deal matters, BBC, 2020. www.bbc.
    co.uk/news/entertainment-arts-52736364 (archived at https://perma.cc/
    P3ZK-NA2R)

11 Statista. Estimated number of podcast listeners in the United Kingdom (UK)
    from 2017 to 2026, Statista, 2022. www.statista.com/forecasts/1147560/
    podcast-reach-uk (archived at https://perma.cc/SXX3-DU2Y)

12 JCDecaux. The advertising bus shelter: JCDecaux's trademark, JCDecaux,
    2014. www.jcdecaux.com/blog/advertising-bus-shelter-jcdecauxs-trademark
    (archived at https://perma.cc/P3YA-4YUJ)

13 Marketcap. JC Decaux SA, Marketcap, 2025. marketcap.company/market-
    capitalization/pa-dec-jc-decaux-sa/ (archived at https://perma.cc/B4GP-MXYR)

14 Statista. Number of digital out-of-home (DOOH) screens in Great Britain from 1st quarter 2020 to 1st quarter 2023, Statista, 2024. www.statista.com/statistics/1050064/digital-out-of-home-dooh-screens-great-britain/ (archived at https://perma.cc/KT9D-WTRB)

15 J Hines. Noticing more OOH travel ads while on the move? There's a reason for that, The Drum, 2025. www.thedrum.com/open-mic/noticing-more-ooh-travel-ads-while-on-the-move-theres-a-reason-for-that (archived at https://perma.cc/CD7W-GLQX)

5

Marketing measurement

Introduction

One of the biggest promises of the internet era was that marketing measurement was going to be revolutionized. The industry had been running for a century or more largely on proxy measures of readership or footfall estimates rather than exact ones. The dot-com era seemed the answer to a lot of measurement challenges for marketers.

When the first banner ads were created in the 1990s, the number of times an advert was shown on the screen could be counted to the nearest one. No more observed numbers, no more annual reader polling or modelled data of views on an advert. Even in a primitive time of digital technology, the ability to count every impression (display of the ad on the screen) was possible. It was revolutionary and raw. And there was no interference from the browser or user cookie settings to blur the data like we have today. The most likely reason an ad wouldn't show was due to a failure of the infrastructure somewhere than anything else!

As I've argued earlier in this book and will do again, this 'countability' of advertising has been a phenomenal thing in some positive ways but it has also fundamentally changed how marketing and advertising is done for the worse.

However we want to view the measurement of our marketing efforts in this more modern era, there will be no escaping the fact that it must be done. Your role and success as a digital marketer will come down to how well you can prove the effectiveness of the work that you are in charge of. If you spend your company's hard-earned marketing budget in the wrong places, it will have not only a detrimental effect on the business overall but also on your and your colleagues' future. This book is here to help you understand what needs to be measured, how to do it and what to do with that information so that you have more good days than bad ones!

The measurement challenge

With measurement being crucial to both business and personal success, getting data collected properly accurately should be of paramount importance. But from my many years of experience, the breadth of marketing measurement carried out by the travel industry is vast. Some travel businesses happily spend on SEO or social media campaigns without the faintest clue if they worked, while some track almost every single touch point and can produce hundreds of graphs on almost every element of their digital journey. In the end, both of these approaches have their drawbacks – either working in the dark or working with all of the lights turned up. It's hard to see what's working with either approach sometimes.

More often than not, when we start to work with clients in our agency, we have to let them know that their measurement set-up is inadequate. Google Analytics isn't counting correctly, they rely on phone calls yet have no call tracking in place or their CRM/booking system doesn't link up to their wider marketing efforts. When one of your biggest outgoing spends as a business is leaking data all over the place, then you've got a problem. Sometimes it's a very big one.

The aim of measuring our marketing efforts is purely to help us understand more of what is going on and then make better decisions. I can't talk about measuring our marketing without referring back to one of the most famous quotes there is in marketing. It is widely believed (though sometimes debated) that early 20th century businessman John Wanamaker said, 'Half the money I spend on advertising is wasted; the trouble is I don't know which half.'[1]

Even in simpler times, knowing what was working was a problem that needed to be solved, and a century later it often feels that nothing has changed! Despite being able to export reports from dozens of sources instantly, it doesn't mean that we have got any data that makes sense. More often than not, more data brings more questions. And that then makes us realize that the numbers we're looking at make even less sense than we originally thought.

Take Google Analytics (GA), for example. When we think about digital marketing across the Western world, we have to talk about GA. It's been the backbone of nearly every digital campaign that I've ever worked on in my career. For over a decade, the reports we looked at in the analytics interface were widely seen as standard and understood by not only marketers but also most business owners, who have been involved in websites in their infancy and were able to make some sense of what GA was telling them. When we looked at our traffic reports and then conversions, it was simple to see that the spend on, say, Google Ads was paying back nicely. 'This is working! Let's spend more!' was the trap that was set by Google and we nearly all fell into it. While the interface of the Google Analytics version known as Universal Analytics (UA) was simple, it was often too simple. By using a last click attribution model, that is to say, the last click that happened before the conversion event occurred, it was very common for Google Ads to get all of the credit for the booking without it necessarily having the biggest influence.

The analogy that I give in my talks is one you can use right now. As you read these words, ask yourself, 'How did I get to where I'm sat right now in this moment?' Unless there are extreme circumstances, the answer is always going to be, 'I walked.' You had to move from one place to another by walking (or pushing yourself if you are in a wheelchair). You may have taken a bus to get your place of work, then perhaps even cycled or got a lift in a car afterwards, before then walking to where you are now. No matter how you travelled, you'll have to have got up from your mode of transport, onto your feet, to then sit down somewhere else.

By looking at the last action only when it comes to measuring things, we miss out everything else that leads up to the final action, which in this case would be nearly all of the transport network! Our pie chart of how people get to their destination would be 100 per cent walking and if we used this data to inform any future town planning, the spaces around us would be incredibly different.

The simplicity offered by the UA version of Google Analytics made it easy to make some decisions but missed out some fundamental issues as just described. In the most recent release of Google Analytics, which was eventually forced on us in 2024, Google Analytics 4 (GA4), the fundamental model of website measurement changed, as did the reporting screens, and as a result, the whole digital marketing measurement world did too. And even now, years on since its initial release, we're still largely struggling to get our heads around it. Despite its name not changing, the product of Google Analytics changed from a fairly simple marketing reporting tool to a proper analytics tool. I have always said that it is a fundamentally different tool but with the same name. This has caused confusion, frustration and many other negative feelings to almost everyone who works with Google Analytics since the new version was released.

If we're being kind, we could say that Google worked really hard on improving the data and reporting in GA4. They knew for a very long time that the UA version had many issues within it, such as how sessions were handled, how to measure across multiple devices and how to handle privacy. All of these issues were thought about and improved in GA4 but the measurement set-up became a lot more complicated, as did the reporting options available. This was because they knew that taking a simplistic approach wasn't the right one nor what some of their bigger clients needed or wanted.

What seemed be forgotten though was that, while GA was the market leader, the vast majority of marketers using it were not hugely clued up on data management and configuration. Our focus is on selling travel, creating cools adverts, testing campaigns and seeing if they work. Most marketers don't want to (or can't) spend time working out how to count conversions by first-time users against general traffic and spend ages to work out what this means. By seemingly designing their flagship analytics tool for a small chunk of powerful users (who I will assume spend the most amount of money on Google advertising products) it has created chaos for millions of marketers across the globe. 'All I want is a report like I used to have in GA, why can't I get that?' is the phrase we still hear years after the launch of GA4. One could argue that in making reporting and data collection harder, in many ways it opens up the chance for Google to blur more data and control the things shown to us for their own ends rather than helping us. Let's not go down that rabbit hole here.

Fundamentally, those that use GA4 have a huge amount more power in their hands to create better data frameworks, capture more reliable information and get better insights. It's just that most travel companies don't have the time, budget or skills to do that and get the most out of this tool.

But getting data and marketing measurement improved should be a necessary goal for every travel business. With so many companies reporting poorly, and still potentially operating in the world of John Wanamaker, there is a fantastic opportunity for you and your business to get ahead of the competition. As mentioned in Chapter 3, nearly all travel businesses rely heavily on Google Ads, Meta Ads and other digital platforms to generate bookings. Over time, the cost to be on these channels only increases.

If we see a 10 per cent increase in our cost per clicks year on year, within seven years our costs will have doubled. By being smarter with our reporting, we're able to not only reduce our ongoing costs, but also pinpoint the phrases, ads and creative that have the most impact and do more of them. This is where we can win more often, get better returns and do better in our jobs. But getting data measurement right is hard to solve as it needs technical assistance and good understanding of not only how data is recorded, but also what to measure and how. As a result, it becomes something that gets overlooked or pushed down the 'to do' list and instead marketers take the route of spending more on media, which potentially makes our problem even worse. It's maybe fair to say that no one in marketing got in trouble for generating more clicks that bring more people to a website, but they potentially did if they spent the same amount on better reporting without having anyone extra come through the digital door.

Best practice measurement set-up

Measuring your digital marketing requires a number of elements working together to get the best view of what's working. Relying on just one or two tools isn't going to give the best perspective over what areas are lagging and which ones are driving your business forward. The utopia we would love to reach is to see each interaction point of a potential traveller with our brand from discovery through to booking and then in trip. Realistically, the only company that has this information to any sort of depth is Google (through Chrome, search, maps, Android and other touch points) but they only ever share a version of this information with us, not the whole view. Therefore, we should be aiming to collect as much information as we can ourselves to get a view of how our users are interacting with our digital outposts, how they are booking and what the value of those bookings are.

There are several technical elements that I believe are critical to success, which are outlined below, roughly in the order in which they are interacted with through the booking journey:

- **Website:** Your website may be many years old but is hopefully built using a modern CMS allowing you full control over all the product content and showcasing all of the travel experiences that your company offers online. Embedded within the loading of each page should be at least one analytics tool which will send as much information back as possible to the data platform to capture data about the visit. If possible, when an enquiry form is completed or online booking made, it should generate a unique ID (as well as ideally capturing a Google Ads Click ID, known as GCLID) which is then recorded both in GA and also in the website database or the CRM, so that a link can be made between the online activity that generated the lead and then any offline activity.

- **Analytics tool:** Google Analytics is the default for nearly all websites across the world still so it's most likely that you have this installed on your website, perhaps using Google Tag Manager to add some additional tracking on top of the standard measures. It's there to measure your website visitors, traffic sources and hopefully booking or enquiry form completions.

- **Phone call tracking software:** A huge amount of travel businesses rely on the phone to speak to potential travellers about where they want to go and deal with any questions about the trips on offer. For some travel companies this can be up to 80 per cent of their enquiries, and for these businesses having a phone call tracking system set up linked to their analytics should be crucial to show how users interact with their marketing prior to picking up the phone. Each user is shown a specific phone number linked to a marketing channel (or even keyword) which, when called, sends information to the likes of GA so that conversions (called key events in GA) can be recorded and attributed to the right source. Not having a phone call system when a notable percentage of bookings are generated through phone calls creates a huge hole in your marketing reporting and should be fixed as a priority even if it comes at a monthly cost.

- **CRM:** When an enquiry is made online, it may (or may not) go directly into a CRM system. For smaller operators, it might still send an email to an inbox where someone might pick it up and then enter the details into another system where it is then progressed. Ideally your CRM would be an off-the-shelf one like Hubspot, Zoho or Salesforce so that it can be customized to meet the needs of the business but also integrated into other systems without lots of extra cost.

- **Enquiry emails and booking confirmation:** Once the potential traveller has been spoken to, an itinerary might be created which might be built in Word and then sent via email as a PDF attachment to the potential traveller, whereby a conversation might happen between two people on email. In an ideal world, any links back to the website would be tracked using UTM codes, which would show the interactions with your emails and website in Google Analytics.

- **Payment provider:** If you allow bookings to happen direct through the website, or for payments to be taken via email links post booking confirmation, then there will need to be some integration with your payment provider of choice and Google Analytics to capture the source and booking value.

- **Booking system:** Once an itinerary or trip has been finalized, it will be entered into a booking system where information on the traveller and their group will be stored, alongside any flight or ancillary details the travellers have picked. For some travel companies this booking system is central to everything and maybe used as a CRM even if it's not as fully functioning as more mature products. Again, linking this back to the original source ID or to the CRM record would allow you to link different touch points of a booking journey together to get a more holistic view of your marketing success.

- **Email marketing platform:** To allow marketing and sales teams to function, an email platform will be in use to allow staff to send marketing communications to new and existing travellers to encourage more bookings and ancillary sales. The data within this system may or may not be linked to booking/CRM systems and may or may not be segmented with attributes like passenger group size, time/location of last trip and various other data points. As before, any link that can be made to booking data will only be advantageous when it comes to segmentation based on lifetime value or other measures.

- **Customer portal:** For those companies wanting to really enhance their digital footprint and improve their customer experience (as well as streamlining their internal operations) a digital 'front end' will be offered to those that have booked via an app or website portal. Customer documentation will either be pushed into here via a clever technology set-up (such as integration with booking system) or occasionally manually uploaded as and when documents are available.

- **Travel concierge app:** While the mobile web is now the dominant platform for nearly all companies, for some travel businesses it makes huge sense to have an app to deliver the best travel experience possible. Dates, flights, itinerary timings, essential paperwork… there are many things needed to get from A to B. Sometimes having everything in one app where documentation can be easily accessed alongside regular updates to both excite and inform your travellers can be of huge benefit. If you have one of these apps, then integrating your GA4 account would be beneficial to see who is using and when. This can then show how engaged your travellers are with the app but perhaps also offer remarketing opportunities further down the line.

Whether you have all or just some of these systems in place, there can be no doubt that it is complex to get even just some of these things working together properly. It requires not only up-to-date technology which, if you are a travel company running for any length of time, may not be the case but also someone who can 'stitch' these things together and someone in senior management who can see the value in creating a connected ecosystem of data. Getting to this point is not easy!

If you don't, then what? The challenge is getting buy in from someone within the company who can understand the value of what you're trying to achieve in a better data set-up and support it with budget or resource to then make it happen (assuming it's not within your control). How do we do that? The best way is to do your own research; look at the companies available who offer services to connect internal data (usually marketing agencies but also advanced analytics software providers) or speak with people in your network who might be able to deliver the work needed that you have identified that needs doing.

Often, I have found that a bigger challenge is having people in marketing roles who understand the value of good data and then having the confidence to then put something better in place. Perhaps this is one of your own challenges. It is not unusual at all as 'data' is something a lot of the marketing community struggle with and part of the reason why GA4 has gone down so poorly. A large chunk of marketers are visually or creatively led rather than data led. The differences between data and creativity are quite big and often a very long way apart. Unless you are in a bigger marketing team, it's unlikely that you're going to have specialisms or additional support to get knee-deep in integrations and APIs to connect data points together. This will then leave it up to you to upskill or, as mentioned earlier, convince someone who can help to provide additional support.

Assuming you can get some of your systems set up, then what should you be aiming for and why? Here are just a few ideas of what a best practice set-up should look like:

- **Modern booking system/CRM set-up:** A proper central data set allows you to see whether Sarah Singh or Steve Smith has booked several times in the last five years, if they bought luxury packages or only booked a discounted trip, and everything in between. A good CRM should allow your marketing teams to properly understand your client base, your best-selling trips, identify potential opportunities and much more without too much fuss.

- **API options:** There will undoubtedly be times when you will need to integrate your details into other systems. The more you allow APIs (external data links within a system) to 'push and pull' data across your business, the greater your 'data surface area' becomes where information can move about. Tools like Zapier.com offer some low-cost, low-maintenance options for many 'off the shelf' tools to work together. If some of your systems don't have APIs, then you will either need to do some manual work to get them to talk to each other or download data to work with it yourself. You should plan to swap that system for another in the not-too-distant future if you are serious about getting better data across your travel business.

- **Data prioritization:** This isn't really a 'best practice' thing per se, but is more of a wider topic around how data is viewed within the business internally. Having the best systems in the world is all well and good but if you just let your team enter data without care or thought, it's not going to bring the most benefit. Collecting good data should be part of a wider culture of prioritizing data to benefit the business, otherwise your team will take the shortest route to task completion. If data entry takes longer than it should, is hard to do or certain data is optional rather than mandatory in places, what is collected will often become worthless and of little use. The mantra of data is 'rubbish in, rubbish out' which is not the case where data is valued.

- **Easy reporting systems:** Having good-quality data going into a simple-to-use CRM or booking system is one part of the challenge; the next is getting it out. Without a clear and clean reporting tool in place that is accessible to multiple people within the business, there is little point to collecting data in the first place. I've seen data get 'locked' in only a few places and only used by a few people for specific tasks. The ideal set-up is to have numerous marketing reports available for you to access and to be able to change as you need without needing any technical skills. Access to similar reports for sales, finance or operations teams should also be available so that everyone can look at the same data sets in ways that benefit them. This is often achieved using Google Looker Studio, Microsoft Power BI or other similar data aggregation tools.

Creating a single source of truth

However many systems you have, however they are linked up and however they are used will always vary. The priority for you in your marketing role is to have a single source of truth for your reporting and data collection. Using the best practice list above, you could have perhaps half a dozen places where customer details and booking data could be recorded. Running a marketing report using one or two of these data sources compared to others could provide you with very different answers around revenue or cost per acquisition. The outcome? Either more questions that can't be answered or, worse still, wrong decisions made which then harm business performance (and potentially your role!).

The holy grail for any travel business is to have a single place that you go to where you can be happy and clear that all your client data is stored and is as accurate as possible. You need to be able to go to one place in your set-up and say 'Yep, Ms Rose and family did travel for a 10 day adventure trip with us and spent £6,783' without having any doubt about the value, trip details or anything else.

If you don't already have it, then your priority should be to have your reporting system set up so that it has data that pulls from different places but is neatly stitched together and presents a customer record with all their data in one single view. This could be address information, historical booking details, revenue information, profitability, marketing interaction points and whatever else you are able to collect that is of use for your teams. Your system should be robust and as real-time as possible so that if you look at the data on a specific customer view, it gives you real-time information rather than something that is a week old. Assuming you can connect your systems using APIs then this should be pretty achievable, but if not, then some manual uploading and downloading of data will be required.

If this is all too hard to achieve in the foreseeable future for you, then where else can you go to base your marketing insights from? If I had to pick, I'd say the booking system is your best source of customer data.

Your booking system is going to be powering a lot of the operations in the business with traveller information, but also historical information such as number of bookings made by a person, products taken, revenue and other areas that can be used for analysis. If this data isn't easily accessible through a built-in reporting tool that you can use, you will need to be able to export data into another system for analysis later (perhaps even Excel). Having access to this data in whatever format you can get is crucial.

Whatever you use as your single source of truth for bookings, it should link up to your internal data and marketing/website data somehow. For us as marketers, we need to understand the interplay between the marketing activity we undertake and how it impacts the bookings made for the business. This is the fundamental challenge we're looking to solve with our data. Having a Google Ads report showing spend without any connection to the bookings made is largely pointless. Unless you have an ecommerce booking system and most of your clients are happy to make a booking without talking to someone, there will undoubtedly be challenges around linking things up. While Google Ads and GA4 can be used to show number of enquiries made, these numbers won't be linked the actual bookings made and so understanding what is driving success at either end isn't possible.

Ten leads from one campaign could all be attracting the wrong type of customer while three bookings from another source could all convert and generate significant profit. Somehow this needs to be understood so that you can spend more money in the right places and less in the bad ones. If you are limited to having a booking system without lots of integrations and APIs within your business, then the one thing you could potentially create is a unique booking ID within your website which is generated when an enquiry is made. This ID should also be pushed to both Google Analytics and the booking form, either into an email or the booking system directly. Your booking system should hopefully allow for custom fields to be created to collect additional information like this. This ID becomes very powerful as it is a common link between the activity online where you most likely spent time or money, and the actual revenue and products booked.

Once a week or once a month, you should be able to get a download from both Google Analytics and your CRM/booking system to allow you to link these data sources together. From here you can start to compare the performance of your different marketing campaigns. Did Facebook Ads actually generate any bookings? Which campaigns from Google Ads bought the most amount of revenue? How many enquiries did we make from the emails sent last month? These questions and more can be answered by having a process like this in place to show the influence of your marketing towards the bottom line. It's worth noting that running these reports together will take time to show value. Sometimes an enquiry made through a website can take many months to come through to booking. Certain types of travel have a long gestation period and so the lead generated in May might not convert to a booking until August.

As I have said in this chapter already, so many travel businesses fail to even have this basic set-up in place. My hope is that after reading this book you will be inspired to do things differently! With so many travel businesses not having the most basic reporting in place, getting it right can bring a big competitive advantage that shouldn't be underestimated.

Modern measurement challenges

Getting our online activities linked up to our real-world performance is something that every travel business should be aiming for. Without at least some sense of how our digital marketing is performing for the business, we're going to be operating in a very old-fashioned way. Spend money, get bookings is an approach that might've worked in the 2000s when buying traffic was comparatively cheap and waste wasn't really noticed. In modern times when every budget is being squeezed and costs increase year and year, we can't operate like that.

Let us say you have got your bookings linked to your marketing activity and you have a better view of the interplay between online and offline going on. From this, though, you see that one particular activity that used to work, now doesn't. Let's pick on email for example. A send each month used to generate a dozen leads which were of good quality. Twelve months later we can only see half a dozen leads, a 50 per cent decrease! What has happened? Has our messaging lost its impact? Has our client base lost faith with us?

While the answer could be one of these things, there are also issues beyond the bounds of your business which are having an impact. As time has gone on through my career, for one reason or another, when it comes to online measurement, things have got more complicated. What was once simple to measure is now complex or not possible.

Sadly, getting a true picture of what is working will only get harder from here. That's not to say you shouldn't be investing your time and efforts to measure your marketing as well as you can. You should. It's crucial to get the best set-up possible to defend yourself against those that want to take your budget away or want to take your market share. A good set-up will help you make the best decisions possible.

How we view the data we look at will need to change, though. It's never going to be close to 100 per cent accurate – it's there to act as a guide to help us in the right direction. Which it probably always has been. It's just that, as time goes on, the strength of the signal we get is weaker than it was previously. Why is this the case? There are several reasons, which I will discuss here. It's important to have a grasp of these issues because they are not widely appreciated or understood and so create confusion or misunderstanding.

Cookies

For many years, cookies (the name for small text files used by internet browsers that store information when a website loads) have been a fundamental part of how tracking worked across the internet. Facebook, Google, Amazon and others have and do rely on these small files to hold information that relates to you on a device to make your life that little bit easier (usually a user ID which they can then link to your profile from their systems). If you use one of these big platforms through your browser and accept cookies, it's one of the reasons why you'll always be logged in and able to access everything without having to login each time.

For cookies to work in this modern era, though, we have to nearly always actively accept them on each website that we visit. When the GDPR came into force in 2018, the use of cookies was never really made explicitly clear. Or rather it was, but a lot of organizations big and small chose at the time to ignore the rules. Any piece of data that was stored which could then be used personally identify someone came under GDPRs remit and so allowing things like user ID, IP address or similar to be stored on someone's machine shouldn't be allowed, by default. If they accept to have cookies used, then it should be made clear to that person that their data would be stored and how it would be used (as well as allowing them to remove that information should they want to).

We spent many hours in our office trying to work out how to advise our clients about what to do about website tracking and the impact this could have on their reporting if cookies were suddenly removed from our data collection processes. Post the GDPR deadline of 25 May 2018, nearly every website carried on tracking everyone as it did before and so our tracking systems carried on working. But as the 2020s went on, cookies got back onto the agenda. While in the UK very few companies have been fined (less than 20 at the time of writing),[2] they did start to offer cookie management options to their users. The reality then, and now, is that cookie management from a legal compliance standpoint hasn't been something most travel businesses have thought about unless they were listed on the stock exchange and had big legal teams. The likelihood of getting fined was still very small and it was better to try to collect data if you could rather than stick to the regulations.

That was the case until 6 March 2024, when Google officially rolled out their 'consent mode v2'. This change stipulated that for Google Ads and Analytics to work effectively, every website owner needed to manage cookie consent properly, which effectively meant website owners needed to have a cookie consent option on their website to allow users to specify which cookies they were happy to have on their device. I still wonder why it effectively took one of the biggest companies in the world to enforce cookie controls onto thousands of websites rather than the legislators of the UK and EU. Was it because Google risked coming under fire from the EU for collecting additional data via cookies and would've been fined? Quite possibly. The EU have generated billions for rightly fining 'big tech' over the years. Or did Google do it because they wanted websites to collect less data to allow them to control more of what is shown in GA4 and to push more businesses to use their data modelling models, thus making things more opaque (potentially in Google's favour) and forcing us to rely on them even more? Whatever the reason, cookie control banners are now the norm for most websites and as such we lose anything from 20 to 50 per cent of the website traffic in our website reporting.

This makes getting a 'true' picture like we had in the early days of the internet impossible and as such we can't even truly know the success of each click we pay for anymore. We're in a world where we must rely on machines to 'fill in the gaps' for us both in terms of click behaviour and also the conversions that we achieve. Whether you're an advocate for more user privacy or not, the reality is that as a marketer, our challenge around reporting continues to grow year on year.

Multiple devices

We live in a world where mobile is the predominant device for website traffic. Since 2024, in the UK (and most of the Western world), more time is spent looking at our mobile screens than our desktop ones.[3] With that said, most people will have either a laptop or perhaps second mobile or tablet available to them for work and personal use. While the average number of internet connected devices per person is at 3.6 across the globe, there are huge disparities by continent, with North America averaging 13.4 and Western Europe 9.4.[4] TVs, smart watches, smart speakers, gaming consoles and many other things allow us to consume content in various ways, all adding complexity to marketing efforts. It's not only the person we need to understand but also their device habits.

Once again, it is the biggest platforms that understand our movements across devices. Google with their logged in account access across Google, Gmail, Maps, YouTube, Drive, Analytics, Android and other touch points can follow us in both our offline and online lives. Meta can do the same through WhatsApp, Facebook, Instagram, Threads and their marketing pixel which is on an estimated 10 per cent of all websites globally[5] (and most likely those are the ones driving leads and ecommerce transactions). Microsoft, Apple and Amazon all have similar tentacles into our digital worlds. All of these big tech companies understand the interplay of devices, locations and interests that we broadcast when we use the internet. As marketers in travel businesses, we have to rely on the data that they provide us with to make our decisions and the data we can see.

While Google Analytics shows us device information and does a good job of stitching together user visits across multiple devices, it is by no means perfect. Users don't care about being logged in, they want to do their task and move on. If someone uses Google to search on one device but not another, we won't see that. If they spend all their time researching holidays on the phone but then decide to book while at work on a new machine with a different account profile we won't be able to see this either. According to research carried out in 2022, the average email user has 1.9 accounts. If we assume that Gmail users carry the same behaviour then it is very possible for someone to be a logged into a personal account on their phone, while at work they might use a different personal or business one.[6]

While we don't want to track every user with every click, it would be great to know if that person who clicked our ad or watched our video on their mobile phone one evening then booked a trip with us the next day. If they move devices or accounts, that link back to the user will be lost and our thread of analysis will be broken.

Did the original PPC click deliver an enquiry for us? We'll never truly know. It's a challenge that I don't think we'll ever crack. When we use the internet, we only think about our task to be done, and as marketers this poses a permanent challenge where things never match up to the real world. We need to remember there are fundamental holes in our data when it comes to analysing our data and success.

Ad blockers

With so many adverts on the internet and so many tracking pixels across so many websites, more and more people are turning to ad blockers to improve their browsing experience and privacy measures. Personally, despite working in the digital marketing industry for two decades, I've been late to install one onto my devices, only having one in place for a few years, mostly just to speed up my browser as I'd had some very slow loading web pages on occasions.

I'm just another user joining a pool of billions of internet users who are blocking ads for various reasons and to varying degrees. Depending on which data set you look at, the percentage of users using ad blockers varies from 31.5 per cent[7] to 42 per cent[8] globally. However you want to count it, it's probably one-third of internet users who are blocking some or all the ads that we put out there and I would expect this number to keep increasing over time. Some ad blockers will simply take the prerolls off YouTube videos while others will mask an IP address, create dummy accounts for people to use while surfing and do a lot of other things to hide personal data.

However ad blockers are used, the net result will be that your tracking numbers aren't going to be as accurate as you'd like and your adverts might not even be seen in the first place, despite your best efforts. As well as not being seen, they potentially may still be charged to you, causing a double pain. The use of ad blockers does vary by age, though, and it shouldn't really be a surprise to learn that younger audiences have more usage than older generations.[9] This is another nuance that you will need to understand when it comes to who you're targeting, how they behave and the impact this will have on your reporting data.

Google Analytics set-up

When Google Analytics 4 became mainstream in 2024, it was something that a lot of marketers were late to pick up on. Only a very small percentage of companies played around with the beta version, and I would imagine those that did were largely nonplussed by the new version – I certainly was. And I think because of this general apathy and dislike towards GA4, the uptake was slow. The analytics and marketing community didn't have lots of good things to say about it, which meant uptake was fairly limited. In 2023, Google set a deadline of 1 July 2024 for UA ceasing to work, effectively forcing us to start using the new version. This at least kicked the discussion of migrating into full swing, but with an official 15-month deadline it was easy for marketers to push it down the to-do list. While nearly every travel company I'm aware of did make the deadline in the end, it didn't mean that the set-up that was live on 1 July 2024 was correct or fit for purpose.

Google offered an automatic migration tool to help speed up the process of migrating settings from UA to GA4 for website managers and did a fair job of putting some better data in place. However, it didn't make the most of the new features available nor did it solve any fundamental problems around how tracking code might've been set up. Data was collected, and at a top level the reporting might've looked fine. Under the hood, though, all sorts of gremlins could be lurking. Cookie consent banners that don't actually consent, tracking working on some pages but not all, code loading in the wrong parts of pages… Bad set-ups didn't become good ones through automatic migrations. And, similarly, even those with IT or agency support didn't necessarily have correct set-ups. New GA code being added to the website might've collected user behaviour but could've bought in double counting for certain measures or more commonly not counted the important things at all. Even as I write this book in 2025, I know of several very large travel websites that turn over tens of millions of bookings that don't have ecommerce tracking set up in their GA4 account, over 12 months since the enforced switch-over date.

With challenges around reporting being a battle for us all, the least of your issues should be your own website analytics set-up. If you're going to collect any digital marketing data, it's important to get your own set-up robust and tested so that you can at least rely on your own numbers for accuracy. The sad truth is that a lot of travel marketers haven't done this diligence and take what they see at face value. If you've never had your set-up double checked by an external third party at least once, then it's fairly likely that you've got an issue somewhere with your tracking, with visits ending up in the wrong channel or key events being counted incorrectly.

The travel tracking challenge

Every industry comes with its own set of challenges when it comes to tracking and marketing. In ecommerce, the starting point for a lot of product searches is Amazon, Google, EBay or perhaps something newer like Temu. As soon as a user goes into a shopping portal, they will be faced with dozens of retailers all competing for the purchase, with price often being a large factor. The result is a slow race to the bottom, with margins being eaten daily as users buy lower prices and advertisers having to pay more to maintain visibility. However, when money is spent on marketing, it's usually pretty easy to see the connection between the click and sale.

In the business-to-business (B2B) world, decisions take months or sometimes years to make. Potential buyers can visit a website today and then not come back again for months, meaning the money spent on advertising can be seen as wasted when it might have been hugely influential.

In the world of travel, we have something in between. A lot of travel decisions are made in weeks or months but typically happen over many touch points in that time. A potential traveller will need to first have a selection of places or destinations that they want to consider, and then start to narrow down specific cities, hotels or places of interest they want to go to. From there, it's then about comparison between various providers before either making a few enquiries or calls or making an online booking.

Various studies have been conducted over the years to look at how travellers search and book their trips. Some of the data points from them are outlined below:

- Google carried our research in 2016 to show a variety of different user behaviours across different booking and travel needs. All of these showed that over a few months dozens or hundreds of Google searches were carried out and hundreds of websites were visited before a booking was made.[10]

- In 2017, a study by Comscore showed a typical 'path to purchase' of 89 days across 34 websites and 182 touchpoints.[11]

- Another study in 2017 by Sojern showed that even a simple hotel booking could take anything up to 127 touch points online.[12]

- A survey across 26 countries in 2019 suggested it takes over 10 hours to plan a holiday as reported by the *Independent*.[13]

- More recently, Expedia Group in 2024 found an average 31 days of inspiration, 38 days of research and 88 pages of planning content are visited to get the booking confirmation.[14]

- In 2024, YouGov found that the typical amount of time to research a holiday is over four months for half of UK travellers.[15]

Whatever version of these statistics we want to use, the booking journey is undoubtedly complex. We can't underestimate the trials and tribulations that a family, couple or solo traveller will go through if they decide to book their own trip online by themselves. It takes many weeks, websites and no doubt plenty of discussions with friends and family, for someone to make up their mind and finally spend their hard-earned holiday fund on a trip away somewhere.

What does this mean for you? We need to appreciate that each paid-for click, advertisement show, video promoted won't always be the thing that gets our booking made. There is a compounding effect to some degree of being there for every part of the journey, rather than just at the end when someone wants to buy. If we can present our trips and brand at the upper end or middle part of the funnel and get travellers to click on us when they are looking around, we have a much better chance of following them through their decision process over time. But this also means that any effort we put into doing that is going to show itself differently in our reporting data.

It might be that some channels, phrases and web pages help to get people interested but don't lead to conversion. Viewed through a conversion-only perspective, many of our efforts might seem a big waste of time or money. But in fact they are critical to our long-term success.

In all these pieces of research, we know that the travel booking journey takes *time*. There is a typically a research phase, a consideration phase, a comparison one and then finally a booking. Each of these stages can each take days or weeks until finally the deposit or full amount is paid. If you look at any marketing diagram trying to explain this process, you'll nearly always see a nice linear funnel going from top to bottom. However, life is rarely that simple or prescriptive. It's usually a mess of thoughts, discussions, searches and then many, many more again!

It wasn't until Google's 2020 article about the 'messy middle' that the process that nearly all of us go through at some point when it comes to purchasing something was finally visualized and discussed.[16] It's a good read and one that has probably not been talked about enough in the marketing world, with the 'funnel' still being de facto.

In the messy middle, research shows that from the point of deciding to purchase something, in our case travel, there are two main phases that users will go through – exploration and evaluation. The first opens more choice, the second tries to narrow it down. But often as choices narrow down, it forces us to go broader again to consider other things. In travel, this could mean wanting to go to a certain location only to find that the costs are too high, or picking a hotel or two to find that they are booked up, or reviewing several travel companies and their reviews before finally making an enquiry. Thinking logically, this approach to purchasing shouldn't really be much of a surprise. Yet it's something that hadn't been properly explained or researched until that paper was released.

For a lot of travel purchases this means showing up a lot and being present through as much of the research and buying journey as you can. I talked in Chapter 3 that channels like social and remarketing don't seem to deliver much in the way of conversions or value, but they can help push some potential bookers through this journey. If someone has narrowed down a list of choices, then it's important that you stay with them through that journey and try to edge them towards selecting you when they click that submit button to make enquiry.

Understanding all of this is hard. In the sections earlier in this chapter, I talked about the technological challenge we have when trying to collect good data that can help us and it is a very real one. Additionally, the standard tools used in measurement, like Google Analytics, have traditionally done a poor job at showing us how users click and go through the journey, instead showing us the last click that generated success.

Google Analytics 4 does a better job of showing us the influence that certain channels have in starting the buying journey, pushing them on and then converting them at the end. But it is still aggregated to 'help' us out without allowing us to get into the detail. To do that, we need separate tools like some of the better CRM ones in the market that track every user interaction. They allow you to tie up all of the previous interactions by a specific user that happened on your website, email or other channels prior to them make a booking or enquiry. Other tracking tools are available that also do a similar job without the need for the CRM element, albeit without being able to tie up multiple devices that a user may interact with.

However you achieve it, though, the more detailed and granular that you can get with your data collection to learn more about how your best or most popular bookings occur, the more insight you'll have about where your marketing investment is paying back. Relying on basic reports which only typically show the last or first click will hide all of the journey and all of the dozens of clicks and weeks of time that happen. The result of this type of approach is most likely a degradation in performance and an increase in cost of your marketing over time. If you can find the resource and budget to introduce better analytical collection and reporting, it's an investment that can pay back well over time.

Different levels of measurement

The 'correct' level of tracking and measurement set-up is going to vary for each travel business. If you are a standard OTA or meta search travel business, then measuring your affiliate links or online conversions should be a lot easier than a bespoke tour operator building specific itineraries with multiple conversion points for your travellers.

Whatever your travel business, there are certain stages of data collection maturity that you should aim for. Below outlines some of the stages you should aim to go through if you've not got a lot set up currently but want to improve. Sometimes travel companies don't know what they don't know so this list aims to show you the art of the possible and the benefits of doing so.

- Basic tracking:
  o You will have a website set up with a basic GA4 installation with the code on every page of your website. This will show what traffic has come into your website in the standard way. If someone completes a form, then a 'key event' will be recorded automatically through the Enhanced Measurement settings.

- o This will give you a top-level view of everything going on but might miss specific channels that are not set up correctly (social, email, etc.) as well as potentially double counting certain events that might be important due to the 'out of the box' settings which are generic and not specific to your travel business.

- Customized tracking:

  - o As above, you'll have GA4 collecting data but might've gone a bit further with your customization to either collect form fills correctly (Enhanced Measurement will only count submit button presses, and so if there are issues with form completion and forms are submitted more than once, you won't be able to tell this) as well as perhaps other 'micro' events such as an availability search to get a deeper understanding of how users are interacting with your website. These micro events can be great at spotting how your users navigate as well as creating potential audiences for remarketing or exclusion in Google Ads.

  - o As an example of this, a travel company we worked with wanted us to push PPC traffic to certain destinations that they had traditionally done well with. However, over time, product had been removed and when users got to the page, only two or three products were shown in a list. This ultimately led to a poor conversion rate and costing the client a lot of money

  - o In GA4 it is possible to show this information by creating a custom GA4 event to count the number of properties shown on a search results page. An Explore report could then be created to show the correlation between the number of properties returned and the conversion rate of the page. If a page only had a handful of results and poor conversion rate, then the PPC could be turned off to save money if we don't have enough product to show them and can't get bookings. Often, we don't know all of the product in our website and so having our tracking tell us what is returned and when, and how this affects our sales, could be incredibly useful.

- Phone call tracking:

  - o If you have any significant levels of phone calls coming into your travel business (let's say more than a third of your leads each month), then investing in a phone tracking system should be your next step in your measurement roadmap. Without knowing where your phone calls are originating from, it's impossible to know how successful some of your channels are.

- o A good phone tracking system will provide you with a tracking script to put into your website that will dynamically change the phone number shown to the website visitor. That phone number will dynamically change to represent the source (or if some extra setting up, even adgroup) that the website visitor last came in from. When they dial that number, it will create a key event in your GA4 account and then route the number through to your call centre.

- o Given how many travel businesses rely on phone call enquiries to power their bookings, the lack of insight into this aspect of their marketing performance is often quite staggering. If you are one of those businesses not tracking calls when you should, then this is a great opportunity to be smarter than the competition! While these tools aren't usually that cheap (coming in at a few hundred pounds a month), if set up and used correctly they could easily save this in reduced media spend. If you can't afford this long term then you don't have to commit to investing in these tools for years; a three- or six-month trial could be enough to start to build out a model which you could then apply going forward (e.g. 1 in 2 calls come from PPC, 1 in 4 from email, 1 in 4 from partners).

- o This approach should also be applied to any offline marketing that you undertake. Having a specific phone number on your printed brochure or print adverts is basic marketing measurement, but again is sometimes forgotten about. If you are using some of your own phone numbers, which can be cheaper to set up than an ongoing phone call tracking system (as well as being more permanent), then make sure that you are able to get a report to show how many times that number was dialled and which source it relates to.

- Advanced tracking:
  - o Taking this a step further, if someone did make an enquiry with you, then you could create an ID for that booking and push into you're your CRM and GA4 at the same time. This would effectively treat your booking website as an ecommerce one where we can see which products are being enquired about. Having an enquiry ID that can be used to link to your online activity to your offline processes to create a continuation of your reporting is vital.

  - o By creating a link between online and offline marketing using a unique identifier, you are then able to get a download from both GA4 and your internal systems to show what enquiry turned into a confirmed booking, to then work out a 'real' ROI from some of our digital (and offline) campaigns. If we can build up a picture over time of what phrases are turning into leads (and ideally the activities leading up to it too) and then into confirmed trips, we can build up a better picture of where our best returns are coming from. If we don't have this link, then we won't able to tie our success back to our spend, which can mean we continue to waste budget on phrases that bring us time-wasters instead of focusing on the ones that drive actual bookings.

o Setting this up requires a small investment upfront to configure GA4 and your website but isn't hugely complex. The ongoing challenge is to do this 'match back' each week or month to link the online conversions to the offline bookings. It is also an ongoing process to look further and further back as some leads can take weeks or months to turn into a confirmed booking with deposit. You will need to update many weeks previous each time, which will affect how you view success of certain campaigns, as it might take a few months to see if they were 'good' or not.

o Having someone who is good with spreadsheets or data systems here is crucial, especially if it's outside of your own comfort zone or you don't have someone internally. Usually marketing or specialist data agencies will be able to either set up and automate this process or offer ongoing support for a fee. While it might cost several hundred pounds or even thousands each month, if you are spending anything over £100,000 or more a year on your marketing budget, it's probably worth the investment. Finding the real 'money' paths and phrases to focus on can hopefully allow you to invest more over time in the right places and cut your wastage without having to increase your budgets.

- Enterprise level:

o Perhaps only once or twice in 20 years have I seen travel clients operate at this level of data reporting and measurement, so this is far from the norm unless you are usually in the tens or hundreds of millions of revenue per year. This level of measurement goes far beyond the advanced set-up and allows for almost every click to be measured and monitored over time and be used to tie together each user's journey from first click to last. Using a complex technical set-up of capturing Google ID (which is each person's unique ID as identified by Google via cookie) from the first visit and then pushing it into a database on each subsequent visit with the date, source and page viewed. Over time, a picture is built up of the multiple interactions that someone will have with the travel business before they book.

o This can then be used to show a variety of things such as length of time from first visit to booking (and trending graphs over time to show booking pattern changes over years), the product someone originally looked at compared to the one they booked, the profitability of each specific adgroup or keyword over time, which adgroups or products are looked and booked (or not) and attribution of all marketing channels over time to help drive smarter investment for the medium or longer term benefit of the business.

o This type of set-up typically needs a dedicated person within the business who not only understands how websites are setup but also how tracking systems work, how data should be structured and then how to present this back to their team visually, which is often the biggest challenge of all. This type of investment is usually needed when the spend on paid media gets above £1,000,000 a year or more although it isn't the norm even at this level. The investment into a person and systems overall might be less than 10 per cent of the paid media spend but the value that they bring should pay for itself either in profitability through increased bookings on more popular or profitable trips and/or savings through cutting media spend which isn't delivering.

o There is a risk for businesses having a single person or handful of people who understand how this set-up works and operates which is hard to mitigate. Some external companies specialize in implementing and managing these types of systems with proprietary software, which is another option. However, that also brings a certain amount of tie-in (it is very hard to move once set up) and usually significant ongoing costs, which is also a factor. There is no definite answer of what is best – it's up to you to decide how valuable a person or system might be and go with that. But if you are able to get to this level of data granularity it can be a huge asset to the business and allow you to make incredibly powerful decisions compared to the rest of your market, ultimately helping to create more profit for longer periods of time.

Whatever version of measurement maturity you're able to get to, there are always ways to improve how and what you track. The job of measuring activity is never finished but there will be a point for your specific business where the investment level will be right so that you don't over-invest in your set-up. Over-investment though is incredibly unlikely as generally travel businesses under-invest in measurement and the typical outcome is poor reporting. This then often leads to the decision to spend more on paid media because 'it works' and marketing measurement is 'too hard'. While that could the right thing to do, it most likely isn't and over time it will create incremental inefficiencies as well as feeding more into the pockets of Google and Meta, which then increases competition in your paid channels and leads to lower profitability over time. Getting value from data is incredibly hard and not all marketers are good with data management and reporting. However, having an awareness of what is possible and the benefits of spending more time getting measurement right should be something that more marketers are aware of. While no marketing measurement platform or set-up is ever going to be 100 per cent accurate, getting it right will increase the validity and usefulness of the signals you're picking up to be more confident in your approach.

Key marketing measurement metrics

Often when I speak at events with travel marketing people they will ask me, 'What metrics and measures should I be looking at?' It's a tricky one to answer as standard because all travel businesses operate differently. The 'It depends' answer isn't really much use, but it always will be the case if we want to be specific. However, most travel businesses have similar marketing approaches and will be looking at the same tools, so I think there are some standard measures you should be looking at regularly to help inform your decision making. I've listed them out below with explanations:

- Engagement rate by channel:
  - It's important to know how well each channel you're spending time and effort on is performing when customers land on your website. Some marketers still report on bounce rate, which is a hangover from the previous version of Google Analytics. It is a negative way of viewing our website visitors, when a better approach is to use engagement rate to see how engaged visitors are with your website (which is either spending over 10 seconds on a website or visiting two pages).
  - If you have an engagement rate of anything less than 50 per cent on a channel then it could mean that you're attracting the wrong type of person to your website, your messaging is misaligned to how they found you originally or your product pages aren't strong enough through things like price, imagery or description. It's worth reviewing both the channel that generated the visit and the most popular pages that they land on to see where improvements can be made.

- Brand vs non-brand performance:
  - o This can be easily seen if you are spending on Google Ads, as you can break down your keyword data by brand and non-brand searches. Brand visitors will nearly always be aware of you prior to visiting your website and so usually behave quite differently, being more engaged and much more likely to convert.
  - o If you're looking at your organic traffic then the way to look brand and non-brand traffic is by looking at home page visits (and any other links that appear when you search for your brand name in the links under your home page on Google – known as sitelinks) against the landing pages which aren't those from the brand search. Typically, the home page and other sitelinked pages (those that show up under your home page on Google when someone searches for your brand) will have the most amount of visits and much different behaviour, so it's worth trying to group these into one bucket and everything else that isn't, into a different one. This can be done in GA4 using the 'custom channel grouping' feature and will help you get a much better idea of how travellers who don't know you and visit you via blog or product pages behave against those that might be visiting just to get a phone number.
- Cost per lead:
  - o We need to know how much it costs on average to generate an enquiry with us, to have at least some view of how effective our marketing is. Looking at this through a last click perspective, though, is fraught with many issues, as discussed earlier in this chapter. Where possible, it's best to look at this through a multi-touch point attribution model, available in GA4 and perhaps in your CRM if you are using something like Hubspot, Salesforce or similar. This will consider all of your clicks, visits and spend that lead to a booking, rather than just the easy-to-track ones. The wider your context for your visits and influence that have helped with lead generation, the better your view is to help keep the ones that help generate initial interest but not necessarily convert.
- Cost per booking:
  - o The thinking here is very similar to the above in terms of trying to understand the value your marketing is bringing but at a deeper level. Having the ability to tie up leads to actual bookings is of huge importance, as discussed, so if you are able to report at this level, you're ahead of most travel businesses!

o Having your booking values available alongside a multi-attribution level is often hard to achieve but, again, if you can get to this point then you can assign business value to marketing efforts, allowing you to cut wasted spend and also show your team the value that your marketing has brought to the business.

o If you can get the enterprise level of measurement described earlier then you'd be able to see how much was spent on each type of booking, how much profit was made on each booking and where your best marketing-to-return ratios are.

- Time from enquiry to booking:

o It's important to know this number as it can highlight changes in your market which could have an impact on how you view success of your campaigns. If you are generating a large amount of enquiries but they are not booking for a while, then perhaps your travellers are becoming more price sensitive or having to deal with other economic or political factors which may or may not affect how and when they confirm their trip. If you see delays around conversion then it can change the success of campaigns to make the view of them potentially longer, or perhaps start to highlight that some element of your offering isn't right.

o Most likely, your CRM or booking system will have some of this information, rather than using GA4, but wherever it is stored, having access to it on a regular basis will help you show anything in your market that you should be aware of (i.e. if times are harder economically, it might take much longer for your lookers to turn into bookers, and knowing this might help you keep your marketing more visible for longer, to increase conversions over time). If you can split out behaviour further by channel or other measures this could again be useful to know, should you want to spend more in one area in the short term but then not see the return for several months.

- Product performance:

o While this isn't necessarily going to change how your digital marketing campaigns run day to day, having some reporting about which products are or aren't selling should be part of your ongoing measurement view. Part of our job in marketing is to spot trends and try to capitalize on them as best we can. If we're spending money promoting a hotel, package or destination and it's not selling (perhaps despite generating leads) then we need to know this so that we can have a discussion with our product or commercial teams to make better decisions internally. Just looking at marketing reports which show leads but don't link to financial success will not help your business or you to progress.

o As with any reporting, the more granular you can get in terms of linking things between channels and performance the greater your understanding will be, and ultimately so should your decision making.

- Demographic analysis:

o The data that we get from GA4 about the different age and gender types who visit our website is all based on modelled behaviour from billions of data points. I have often been assumed to be female by Google due to some of my hobbies, such as cooking, exercise and other interests I have, which the machine will incorrectly label. How much we trust Google's reasoning at an individual level is always open for questioning, but the overall consensus in the marketing community is that demographic analysis is a useful (if sometimes fallible) measure.

o If we know that GA4 has a lot of inaccuracies, we know we can truly rely on the accuracy of our booking data (or lead booking data) in terms of gender and age. Confirmed booking data will always be 100 per cent accurate if linked to passport data, and so should be used as your go-to for knowing who is booking your trips. If you're able to understand the gender, age and location of who is booking your trips, then this can help with your paid media campaigns as well as improving your landing pages, social and email posts by making everything that much more relevant.

- Repeat booking rates (by channel):

o In Chapter 3 we covered different channels and what they should ideally be used for. Some channels might be bringing in lots of bookings but then don't lead to anything in the longer term. A great measure to understand is how many users book trips through one specific channel and they then go on to book again.

o One travel client ran a campaign with an affiliate website helping to sell lots of spare inventory at discount one year, which helped them increase their revenue with some small increases in profit. However, further analysis showed over time that these travellers were only in it for the deal and didn't then come back and book again over the years that passed. That channel didn't deliver over the long term and potentially harmed the brand image by showing that discounted prices could be achieved if they waited long enough.

- Revenue attribution across channels:

  o This type of reporting is going to be available if you're able to track your bookings back to the overall behaviour of each traveller over time. This is only realistically possible using CRM systems that capture every opted-in website visit and can piece this together over time. If you have this then the ability to show all of your revenue over a 3–12 month period against the activity and spend of each channel is a very powerful way to look at how well your channels have performed and contributed to your business success. If some of your channels create a lot of 'noise' (for example blog traffic or email clicks), but don't help to convert lookers to bookers, then you can start to treat your email lists differently or change your SEO focus. If you are running a basic GA4 set-up and have bookings separate to digital marketing activity then you're only going to be able to crudely correlate the two, which could miss out large amounts of detail that could make all the difference.

Summary

Knowing what is right for your specific travel business and for you personally is always going to be subjective. If your travel business is small and has limited plans to grow, a basic approach to measurement might be sufficient. My best guess would be that that doesn't apply to you, which is why you're reading this book! You want to improve your digital marketing knowledge and skillset, so the aim of this chapter is to discuss the art of the possible and outline the benefits of doing so.

It is a sad truth that the digital marketing world is only getting more complicated and more competitive. Budget, attention and data are all in a constant battle with not only other travel brands but also other sectors. To win, we have to be smart. And, in my experience, those that have better data collection and better data analysis tend to win more often. Most of the travel industry has a poor view of what is driving their success, which opens up a huge opportunity to improve. No digital reporting set-up is ever going to be a 100 per cent true version of events, but if you can improve your perspective of performance by seeing what is possible then you will undoubtedly increase in marketing performance over time.

Notes

1   Quote Investigator. Advertising is based on one thing: Happiness. And do you know what happiness is? Happiness is the smell of a new car, Quote Investigator, 2022. quoteinvestigator.com/2022/04/11/advertising/ (archived at https://perma.cc/F294-C9RW)

2   Enforcement Tracker. GDPR enforcement tracker, Enforcement Tracker, nd. www.enforcementtracker.com/ (archived at https://perma.cc/WE6Z-VFA6)

3   Statcounter. Desktop vs mobile vs tablet market share United Kingdom, Statcounter, 2024. gs.statcounter.com/platform-market-share/desktop-mobile-tablet/united-kingdom/2024 (archived at https://perma.cc/66XD-B2PA)

4   A Fleck. Overconsumption: The growing desire for ever more devices, Statista, 2024. www.statista.com/chart/32691/average-number-of-devices-and-connections-per-capita/ (archived at https://perma.cc/73WA-PP57)

5   W3Techs. Usage statistics and market share of Meta Pixel for websites, W3Techs, 2025. w3techs.com/technologies/details/ta-facebookpixel (archived at https://perma.cc/Z3BA-HQ2Z)

6   Radicati Group. Email statistics report, 2018–2022 executive summary, Radicati Group, 2018. www.radicati.com/wp/wp-content/uploads/2018/01/Email_Statistics_Report,_2018-2022_Executive_Summary.pdf (archived at https://perma.cc/N8HL-LNPR)

7   Backlinko. Ad blocker usage and demographic statistics, Backlinko, 2004. backlinko.com/ad-blockers-users#ad block-top-picks (archived at https://perma.cc/H5EV-V6RV)

8   A Crossland. Ad blocker statistics 2024, 2024. www.b2.ai/ad-blocker-statistics-2024/ (archived at https://perma.cc/EJ9W-Y78W)

9   Statista. Share of adults who used pop-up or ad blocking software in the United Kingdom (UK) as of April 2024, by age group, Statista, 2025. www.statista.com/statistics/875604/ad-blocker-users-in-the-united-kingdom-by-age-group/ (archived at https://perma.cc/D9LR-YANL)

10 Think with Google. Micro-moments: Reshaping the travel customer journey, Think with Google, 2016. think.storage.googleapis.com/docs/micro-moments-reshaping-travel-customer-journey-b.pdf (archived at https://perma.cc/K48W-SVDM)

11 TripAdvisor Insights. Worldwide travel path to purchase 2017, TripAdvisor Insights, 2018. www.tripadvisor.com/TripAdvisorInsights/wp-content/uploads/2018/03/comScore-worldwide-Path-to-Purchase-2017.pdf (archived at https://perma.cc/M7ZH-YZNN)

12 Sojern. Sojern and FASTBOOKING reveal complex travel path to purchase can encompass 735 touchpoints, Sojern, 2017. www.sojern.com/press-release/sojern-fastbooking-reveal-complex-travel-path-purchase-can-encompass-

735-touchpoints (archived at https://perma.cc/XU36-GTDV)

13 R Knight. Average person spends 10 hours planning their holiday, survey claims, *Independent*, 2019. www.independent.co.uk/travel/holiday-booking-planning-travel-survey-tourist-a8801211.html (archived at https://perma.cc/W88Z-LM6E)

14 Expedia Group. The path to purchase, Expedia Group, 2023. partner.expediagroup.com/en-us/resources/research-insights/path-to-purchase (archived at https://perma.cc/W28N-YFH3)

15 J Fernandes. Travel booking trends: How far in advance do Brits plan? YouGov, 2024. business.yougov.com/content/50712-travel-booking-trends-how-far-in-advance-do-brits-plan (archived at https://perma.cc/MR5D-RN5B)

16 A Rennie and J Protheroe. How people decide what to buy lies in the 'messy middle' of the purchase journey, Google, 2020. business.google.com/uk/think/consumer-insights/navigating-purchase-behavior-and-decision-making/ (archived at https://perma.cc/86TP-23SU)

6

How to avoid making marketing mistakes

Introduction

You will never have a 100 per cent success rate when making decisions in your marketing role. Every single person in every single job has made many decisions that didn't work out, pushed for projects that were non-starters and assumed activities would deliver bookings, only to find that they didn't. Mistakes are part of everyday life and it's fine to make them. I know I've made hundreds my career and no doubt you have, too.

While mistakes are often an opportunity to learn, in a high-pressure industry such as travel where often our target audiences are only 'in market' and ready to book for a few months at a time, it does mean we need to get things right more often than not. Through this book I've talked about all of the areas that I feel are important to focus on when it comes to marketing. Surely if you just do all these things, your marketing results will improve, right? I'm very confident that they will. I wouldn't be writing this book if I didn't think that I could offer you some value from my own learning and experiences!

However, doing what has been done before will only get you so far. There will be certain times in your career where it will not be obvious as to what the right thing to do is. You will perhaps need to read articles on LinkedIn, go to conferences, watch videos or do a whole load of other activities to take your knowledge further. There is no doubt in my mind that some of what has worked well in digital over the last 20 years will have less impact in the next 20.

How do we make sure that the activities we work on now are going to lead to success? How do we stay sharp in our role to find opportunities in the future to learn and evolve? And, perhaps most importantly, how do you prevent mistakes that others in the industry have done which have been the end of their roles in a company or even damaged the company itself? Working in a marketing role is probably never going to lead to the end of a travel business operating – there are hundreds of other external factors that lead to the demise of a travel business. But getting marketing wrong can certainly lead to some very poor outcomes if the wrong decisions are made. The aim of this chapter is to give you some key areas to think about and focus on when it comes to decision making, so you can learn from others' mistakes and not make them yourself!

Relying on others (or not)

As you progress in your marketing career, you will undoubtedly take on more responsibility from either those above you or those around you. Either way, as time goes on and you learn more about the inner workings of your business and travellers who book with you, you will have more input and more opportunities to influence. Perhaps if that's still a little way off, you will probably have to work alongside other colleagues, freelancers or agency partners to make things happen.

When it comes to progressing your marketing career, the first person that you must think about is yourself. Only you are going to truly drive your career forward in the direction and speed that you want. Having a manager or boss who is supportive, caring and positive is always a huge benefit, but those people are not always readily available. You're going to have to work with whoever is around you for the foreseeable future, so how can you make things work with them? Getting what you want from those around you will always need to be done on a case-by-case basis – each situation will always be different. Whatever you can make work will have to do for now but with an aim of seeing improvements over time.

In a marketing team of more than one person there will be a division of roles, decision making and responsibility. And this is where you need to understand the role that you play in the team and what others do, too. Perhaps you have a manager role, looking after one or two others in your team and reporting to the owner or MD of the company. Or perhaps you are one of many in a larger team, each looking after a specific area of digital or broader marketing, to help a marketing leader in their role of spending millions of pounds each year to grow the business with ambitious targets.

Whatever the situation, your role and other roles should be fairly defined. How do you know what the others in your team are doing and if they are doing the right thing? This usually shouldn't be the thing you spend too much time thinking about – there should always be more than enough to get on with without worrying about what Sarah and Steve are doing all day long. But if you're smart, you will pay attention to things around you. Obviously, focus on yourself first, but also get a sense of everyone else in the business and those close to you. Are they friendly? Are they smart? Are they ambitious or just happy clocking in and out each day? It's not really on you to judge everyone's motivations, they do their thing, you should do yours. But it's always worth paying attention to how capable those that have an impact on you and the business are. And my first tip of this chapter is to never assume that everyone knows what they are doing. It might sound harsh to doubt those around you. However, having a sense of your role, others around you and if they are doing the 'right' thing is at least worth trying to develop and hone.

How do you build this sense of 'good enough' in the activities you're doing and the skills you have in your team? I think that there are two areas – experience in your and other roles and a curiosity about the things that are around you. The first one is going to be hard to achieve if you've only got a few years of experience under your belt. You're not going to know whether the investment that someone decides to make into a printed brochure for your peak booking window is a good one or not if you don't have first-hand experience of this from previous roles – and no one should expect you to. You can obviously go back to your target audience and the research that has hopefully been carried out to work out if the activity matches the market. But sometimes there will just be others in your team who know more and know what works.

Which is where the second part comes in: being curious. Hopefully, the culture within your travel business supports open questions from anyone in your team to ask, probe or find out more about the things that go on. I know that in bigger companies, being open can sometimes be hard when there are internal politics at play and various hierarchies that need to be navigated, so how you ask these questions in a way that is accepted and 'works' will always be a challenge. However you ask, the main thing to remember is why you're asking, which is to build more knowledge of the elements going on around you and to help the business. Good marketing people will do their job and stick to the tasks and activities given to them. Excellent marketers will go beyond this in their own time, reading up on things that are around their current work but help to broaden their horizons. They will read books, watch videos, listen to podcasts and sign up for newsletters that are not necessarily within their specific skillset right now, but branch out into other areas.

By leaning on your own knowledge, by being inquisitive and building relationships in a positive way that helps yourself and also others in your team, you will build greater awareness of the things that are happening to help ask better questions and reduce the chance of mistakes happening. If something does happen in your marketing team or with certain activities, then you have the chance to share some thoughts that might make a campaign a success rather than a failure or stop yourself or someone else in your team from spending budget on something that isn't going to deliver a positive result.

As an example of this, a travel company we spoke with many years ago came to us in a panic at the end of January. Their peak sales time had been very disappointing, and they had missed their revenue target by quite a big margin, meaning that their sales team were really concerned about how they were going to hit the targets set for the financial year. The peak booking season had largely passed without anything like the bookings they would expect or, more pressingly, had forecast. They wanted our help to turn things around as soon as we could, so our first port of call was to review their PPC account and make some changes. Within a month or so their sales were back on track, as well as starting to show signs of growth. A few months later we took on their SEO activities too, to help them boost their search presence further, which helped them get better sales for the peak campaign the following year.

Despite our best efforts, it just wasn't possible for the client to make up for the big losses that were seen in the first few months of that year. As time went on, we understood more about the history of the client and their previous agencies. The previous marketing director was brought in from outside of travel and was given a large amount of control to spend their marketing budget in the way that they wanted. Unfortunately, that person was best friends with someone who ran a print marketing agency who advised them to turn off their PPC spend in the three months leading up to Christmas as 'it doesn't convert in that time so is a waste. Better to spend your money on print brochures instead.'

While for some travel clients this could perhaps be the right course of action, for this particular one, where their audience was very digitally focused, it wasn't. The printed brochures landed but didn't lead to enough calls being made. Once we had analysed the data from their bad year against previous visit, booking and spend patterns, it transpired that while PPC (and SEO) didn't convert in the run-up to Christmas, it did get people onto the website and to look around. These visits were used to inspire them as to what was on offer and what a potential traveller could look forward to for their summer holiday next year. The crucial three months leading up to Christmas were when their audience was looking but not booking. By turning off a big chunk of their marketing in advance of the booking time of year, they allowed their competitors to be visible, inspire the market and take a larger chunk of bookings when the purse strings were released.

It was an expensive mistake.

It happened because the agency making the recommendations did so to most likely suit their own needs (in the short term at least – they weren't contacted again!). It happened because the marketing director/manager didn't question the rationale behind the decision enough. It happened because those in the marketing team weren't consulted enough or weren't clued up enough to challenge the decision. It happened because there wasn't enough customer insight or data available to validate or back up the decision to cut PPC spend for three months. All of these things could've been avoided and should've been, or at the very least challenged more. The decision to save £10,000–£20,000 in the short term cost as much as £100,000–£200,000 in the mid term.

It is very easy to be complacent in our roles and think 'That wouldn't happen here', but stories like this happen all too often. When a new tool, channel or app comes along and is the talk of the marketing town, others above or below you may be convinced that it's worth investing in. But if you blindly take someone else's word for something you run the risk of being the next person to spend money in the wrong place and potentially cost yourself or your company a significant loss. The big tech platforms spend millions of dollars each year on 'education' and 'client support' and while there is some good in what they share in terms of what is working, there is also a very big bias. Time and time again, bigger agencies will go to the latest webinar or take phone calls from account reps who then push the latest new way of doing something based off a case study or two with a FMCG company who spend millions of dollars in a few weeks on a completely different audience. Many less savvy digital marketers will then do what the platform says because they don't challenge or think things through enough, and within a few weeks new campaigns get created and tens of thousands of pounds can be spent with little to no return to show.

If using new channels or campaign types through big platforms is within your team or within your agency, and you have any remote connection in your role to the money being spent, it's worth listening to what's being recommended to see if it makes sense and if you feel you can, sharing your thoughts in a constructive way. It's sometimes hard to 'get ahead' of these decisions in larger teams to stop them happening, but if it is too late to undo decisions then your next best option is to listen and learn the lessons of any good or bad outcomes.

If you are the one to make a decision and don't have any prior knowledge or experience to lean on, then speaking to your peer group is an option, as is speaking to others in your team about the risks of moving budget into new channels or increasing spending. Having a rounded discussion with those who have an interest in your marketing efforts (or even those that don't sometimes!) about the pros and cons can then help to make better decisions by considering new angles that you might not have thought about or preventing errors happening from the off. If you're struggling for some-one in your team or externally to do this role, then this could be where the large language model (LLM) chat options can help to at least provide a chal-lenge to your thinking.

The point here is to have an opinion and be curious. Do you own research and try to make the best decisions yourself, and help others around you as best you can. Following advice blindly from others, be those the big plat-forms that ultimately want more of your money or in your team who might have the wrong motivations, can really trip you up. Develop your sense for good and bad by reading, listening and asking, and in time you'll make far fewer mistakes.

Being blasé about data

One of the things that continues to interest me about the travel industry is the complexity of the market. While on the surface, it might seem easy and straightforward to book a holiday or adventure, it never is. As I've high-lighted a few times, the journey to travel is complex and long. We might assume that it's a lot easier to say work in ecommerce or FMCG sectors where someone might see a product or ad on social, click to a website and purchase it instantly. Every touch point seems much simpler and trackable, but while that *might* be the case in some instances, it doesn't necessarily mean it is easier. Getting noticed on social takes a lot of effort, the ecommerce landscape is dominated by Amazon and Google, each year costs for clicks get pressured and social channels can make or break a product overnight. It's not quite as easy as some of the marketing case studies make it out to be.

But with that said, travel is by a lot of measures harder, which for me is part of the attraction; I like to solve complex problems! The power of collecting good digital and marketing data is paramount and as someone who has always been very comfortable with numbers, I find it a great subject of interest. But I have realized more and more as time has gone on that I am not in the majority. While the average GCSE grade for maths has gone up in the last few years in the UK, it has historically been behind and is still not above English, which suggests that our love of numbers isn't as great as it of words (or pictures).[1]

This is made perhaps worse in the travel industry, particularly where a lot of the owners, senior management and leadership come from being 'on the shop floor'. Their first start in travel might've been running tours or being in customer service, or another role that perhaps wasn't driven by numbers or analysis. Their focus, very rightly, might be on the customer service delivered on your tour, giving great advice when speaking to someone on the phone or any other touch point, if that is their area of expertise. Because of their background, they haven't then prioritized marketing in the traditional or holistic sense, instead just doing things that 'work' without being hugely proactive with planning or data. There is absolutely nothing wrong with this approach and I know of so many fantastic travel businesses that have been built this way. Realistically, though, it will only get you so far. And, as time goes on, and more and more digital marketing is machine- and data-led, it's not going to deliver.

The one area that is often a blind spot, or perhaps just not seen a priority, for a lot of travel businesses is around data. Data prioritization in established travel businesses which are tied into multiple complex systems, have data agreements with third parties and various people across the business with different reporting needs, can often be poor. The ability or will to collect better data which can be used by marketing teams is often not very strong. These issues can sometimes be rectified and improved over time. But without expertise either from in-house or via external support, it's usually hard to bring the data collected to life and tell better stories.

This can often be a cultural challenge within travel businesses, perhaps even the one that you work in, and can mean that the marketing function is on the back foot. Either senior marketing people are not data-focused in order to fit in with those around them, or the challenge internally to make data more of a priority is too hard. Regardless of how severe either or both of these aspects are, if those in charge of marketing or at a senior leadership level do not properly understand the real value of data or, as I've said, prioritize it to help the whole business, it's going to be a real struggle to make your marketing work, particularly in these modern times.

It's not to say that marketers with a more creative focus aren't important or can't drive success – they absolutely can. But, in my experience, and as time goes on, the marketers that don't have a good understanding of how data is collected and linked within their businesses tend to struggle. The net effect over time is that costs go up to achieve the same result, market share is lost and margins start to erode.

The number of times I speak with new travel businesses, even at the multimillion and global level, who have poor data and attribution is quite stunning. They had a business model that worked well in 2015 and seemingly haven't changed much in that time. And this means that they just don't care about even basic things like accurately measuring GA4 key events or having digital channels collecting the correct data. Seeing 'not set' in GA accounts for a third of all traffic, totalling millions of visits and conversions, is something that I really didn't expect in the 2020s when the industry has spent years talking about the importance of data and analytics, but it happens time and time again. Not only is this data not helpful in the long term, as you can't make any prediction based off historic incorrect data, it's also awful for short-term decisions too. It takes time to build robust data capture, fix analytics to unpick things and get data lined up properly. If you have found issues with data collection in any part of your business, then in my experience there are very few shortcuts to fixing things. It often means many more months operating 'blindly' until your collection processes get sorted and data is correct, but at least you're on the right path.

What does having poor data ultimately mean? It might be that travel companies with poor data can still get away with it for a few more years. But when the graphs start to plateau or decline, they will look to data to try to find out the reasons why and will be clueless. Even if marketers are using data now but it's inaccurate or it doesn't link to commercial success, they will be wasting budget, and again be on a long-term road to decline.

If this describes the business you work in now, and you can see this apathy towards poor data across your business or you're just not getting anywhere, then one of your key roles is to make the case to those that can make decisions to change things. This is never easy, particularly if the culture internally is one of not being data focused, or budgets are tight to find the money to invest.

It might be that you have to have the same conversations with your team for months or even years until things change. No one would like to be in that situation but you need to stand your corner and ideally build up the story as time goes on to counter this – collect case studies from conferences, send links to articles which are relevant or just emphasizing the poor data that you have to work with by highlighting all of the errors and what they don't allow you to do, i.e. 'I can't tell you how to improve our PPC spend as 35 per cent of our visits are being miscalculated.'

There is a very fine line which needs to be walked between sounding like a broken record, and being passionate about making things better. Reporting to your manager month after month that you can't do your job properly due to poor data quality most likely isn't going to go down well. Teams that are proactive rather than pessimistic will always win. So, if things aren't going to change anytime soon, then you will need to work in a softer way over a longer period of time and build on whatever good data you do have. But that doesn't mean you have to give up. A culture of poor data can be turned around over months and years, and as long as you keep up the fight then you will be on the right path to success in the long run. But to turn a blind eye to the data challenge and pretend it doesn't exist will only making things worse as time goes on and make your job harder as a digital marketer.

Get out and about

It's hard to say if other industries get so hyped up so often about new things, but the marketing industry (and travel to a lesser degree) has a very bad habit of finding new things to talk about every year which are heralded as the saviour of lots of marketing (and sometimes the world's) problems. There have been so many new ideas and technologies that have been hyped, talked about for a few years, then completely disappeared from the media landscape – voice technology, blockchain and metaverse, to name just a few. In travel, it's a similar although less severe issue of hype, with words like 'bleisure' (mixing business and leisure time on holidays) and 'baecation' (going on a romantic trip with your partner) being flagged in the press as 'new trends' that travel companies need to jump on. There will always be something new that someone somewhere needs to write about to try to stay relevant or sell some clicks.

In my younger days I very much fell into believing the hype of a lot of the things I read or heard at conferences. Surely the person on stage with 20 years more experience than me must be right? Why else would the conference organizer put them in front of hundreds of people if they didn't have a valid point or something to help us in our jobs? As times gone on, I've realized there can be many reasons why someone is on stage or has a feature in a travel publication, and often it's not because they are right. It could be because they have paid to be there and have an agenda to share, they're from a 'cool' big brand, they know someone in the industry who can get them exposure or they have something to sell.

While reading marketing articles on an ongoing basis is essential to your own development and therefore to the success of your travel company, it is no bad thing to maintain an air of scepticism about what you're reading. It's always worth thinking about what's in it for whoever is telling you the words you are reading (with the exception of what you're reading now of course! This is a book to help you, not sell to you!). The ability to perceive what is good to know and focus on is something that develops over time, and if you're still in the early days of your career this might be harder.

The big tech platforms are particularly good at sending their teams into the world to showcase the latest updates to their platforms to audiences of travel marketers who are always on the looking for opportunities to help them sell their trips. We're right to listen to what they have to say but must overlay this with our own experiences and those who are in similar roles. There does seem to be a chunk of the marketing world who will almost blindingly take information from others and then apply it either too fast or too much in their marketing efforts. Larger agencies particularly tend to be oversold to, which then impacts the performance of their clients, but it does apply just as much to younger or smaller agencies, too. They will often make decisions about how to invest Meta or Google budgets based on the most recent 'account call' which then often isn't the best move for their clients and fails to deliver results that probably weren't ever there in the first place.

You should take the information from others and apply it to your own situation or audience. I wrote about this in Chapter 3 with my Mum Test, which is to say, if we're being told that the new shiny thing is X or Y, ask yourself, can I see my mum or dad doing or using what is being said? Looking back at the hype of voice search and smart speakers, I always held reservations if they were going to be as popular or impactful as was being told month after month in the marketing world. I just couldn't see my parents using a voice speaker in any meaningful way. Smart speakers are now largely used to ask for a Beatles song to be played or to find out the weather tomorrow, but that is largely it (and it seems that was the case for nearly all smart speakers in the end as the Alexa development team got downsized over time).[2] When you're being told by the big tech platforms in direct calls, your agency or someone on stage that a new feature is available and can showcase an uplift in conversions of 11 per cent, ask yourself if that is replicable for your travel business. Is this an example that is relevant and you can learn from, or one that would never work in your niche travel company? Talk to those around you and find out who else has had first hand success that can be applied to your situation.

Not making mistakes here is also linked back to Chapter 2, where we looked at the importance of your target audience. While the Mum Test is relevant perhaps as a more universal principle, it's not applicable to every scenario. If our target audience is families in their 30s or 40s with young children, then how they behave will be different to how my or your parents will behave. In this instance your Mum Test shouldn't necessarily be thinking of your own parents or family, but instead the families you want to target. Observe them as best you can. When you're in town or at an airport, study them carefully in terms of the brands they wear, the apps they're using (without staring too much!) or the books, magazines and newspapers they're reading. If these are your target audience then the more you know about them, the more likely you are to make the best decisions to empathize with them, speak their language and get their enquiry. The closer you can get to your audience, the better your marketing senses will improve. Basing all your marketing ideas and decisions on what you read online is, I would suggest, not applicable to the specific challenges you will face or the audience you want to hone in on. The more you get out and about, the much less likely you are to make mistakes.

> To leave you with some inspiration on the power of being close physically to your customers, let's look at Bernard Arnault. While nearly all of the founders or CEOs of the big tech platforms are well known around the globe due to their fantastic wealth, Bernard is far less well known. But as CEO of LVMH (Louis Vuitton Moet Hennessy) he has amassed a net fortune of over $100 billion as of 2025, making him one of the richest people in the world.[3] While his business acumen cannot be denied, one of the things that has helped him over many

years is his obsession with detail in every business he owns and runs. And this comes from being on the shop floor every Saturday (even after decades in this job), observing his clientele, paying attention to their movements, their clothes, their chat, and getting to know them as well as he can (as well as keeping an eye on his team no doubt).

In being close to his audience each and every week, he's developed a sense of where things are in the world. Not physically, but through evolving tastes in fashion, in technology, in what makes his clients tick. He knows his business not through checking on dashboards (although I'm sure many in his team do!) or reading reports but through observations and serendipitous chats. As digital marketers, we often spend most of our days behind our laptops posting online, attending virtual meetings or producing reports. It's easy to get lost on social media or spend too much time in our inbox. But the more time you can spend away from your screen and where your travellers are physically, the better it'll make your marketing efforts.

Arnaud has made being close to the customer an art form and one that we could all learn from.

Overcoming the HIPPO

I first came across the HIPPO after attending a talk on project management nearly a decade into my career. What has a HIPPO got to do with project management? Well, nothing if you're thinking of large river-dwelling animals. But HIPPO in the business context stands for HIghest Paid Person's Opinion. Ultimately, what does your boss or manager think, and are they the ones making the decisions on things or not?

If you've not heard of the HIPPO, then you will have no doubt experienced it at some point in your life. It'll be those situations where you have worked so very hard on a project or piece of work, gone to great lengths to get all of the research and ideas checked (and double-checked), only to then present it to your bosses and get lots of 'helpful' ideas that completely go against everything you've researched. The person who has the highest title/salary/length of service will come along and, like a hippo, smash through things with their own personal thoughts or preferences, which others then give way to. If you've been on the end of this situation, you will know just how disheartening or upsetting it can be when you've had lots of very good and sensible work overruled on what might appear to be the whim of one or two out-of-touch people.

A mistake here is to ignore what the HIPPO says because they are just going on 'gut' instead of thought or research. While a lot of these conversations do end up sounding like someone picking an image or marketing plan based on what they like to do most, there can sometimes be a chunk of truth in what they say. While the HIPPO might be noisy, direct and sometimes obnoxious, they will probably have been up and down the business river several times and know what is needed to help the business and the clients. They may not have the data to back up their point of view but there may be something that is of use from their many years of experience that you might've missed.

That's looking positively at the HIPPO situation. There are times, though, when the HIPPO is completely wrong. 'We need to have an app!' was a common comment I would hear in the 2010s. These days it might be 'I don't believe in this AI thing', or the opposite, 'We have to ditch everything and use AI for every part of the business.' Often the HIPPO will want to be big and bold on things and not spend the time to work through the nuance of the situation or think about the challenges or costs involved.

Your job when trying to overcome the HIPPO, like everyone in your team, is to try to understand them, their motivations and how best to get the attention to try to win them over. Some digital marketers have a love of data and gain insights from the reports we read and the tools that we use each and every week. Marketing plans will take weeks or months of graft, research and planning to get to a point of being useful and helpful to the business. If you are trying to get buy in from those above, often those people will not think or react in the way that you do. They might be people that thrive on feelings, instinct or big ideas rather than lines in a long planning document. Maybe it's the other way around and you've tried to pitch a big idea to them without giving them any detail at all about why your idea is so great. If you are to make your ideas come to life, then you must get buy in and the way to do that is to 'sell' it to your HIPPO or those that can make things happen in a way that they understand.

Think about it as a marketing and sales plan with an audience of one. What does that audience want? To look good to their boss? To leave a positive mark on the business? To get a salary increase? To sell their business in three years' time? What makes them tick? Is it excitement? Or granular detail? Or helping others?

Having a plan for your plan to get sign off in the way that you believe is best for the business is a big part of making marketing work which I think is often overlooked. Just because you think your ideas are great and are well researched, it doesn't always mean that others with very different agendas and ways of thinking will go for it. Sometimes getting your ideas agreed to will take months of hard work internally. It could be planting the seeds of ideas with influential people who can talk to your HIPPO. It could be drip-feeding information over a period of weeks with links or headlines or videos of things to them that back up your overarching point.

Let's say you want to invest in a new email platform. You might start sharing case studies from your chosen provider or highlight that a competitor is using it and seen great success. Or you could get others in your team to be vocal to your HIPPO about how bad your current set-up is so that the message comes from more voices. There are many tactics you can deploy (all in the interest of progress, of course!) to try to make things happen. Each situation is going to be on a case-by-case basis in terms of getting buy in to make positive changes.

But the overarching point here is that just having good marketing ideas isn't always going to make them happen. Being aware of the structure of your company and the motivations of those around you, and having an idea of how to 'play the game', is extremely important. If you don't push back then you can fall into the mistake of going along with things, the wrong path being taken and ultimately it coming back onto you when things don't work out.

The HIPPO will happily push their own agenda but if things go wrong can sometimes push back on others (or you) to pass on some of the blame. To avoid this happening, it's important to try as hard as you can to get your own ideas heard and to get buy in so that you have as much control as possible throughout your process. And when things do work out, it's also your job to shout about all of the successes you have to help build more trust and confidence in your abilities! Eventually you can tame the HIPPO and use it to your advantage.

Short-term thinking

We live in a world where nearly everything is accessible through the touch of a button. Need an answer to a question? Press a button. Want to watch a film? Press a button. Feeling hungry? Press a button. For the younger generation, this is the world and always has been. For others, there was a time before this where things required more effort, time and perhaps even care. If you wanted to find out about the latest places to visit, you had to watch programmes, read magazines and talk to people of interest who knew about their subject. Now, we press a button and get whatever it is given to us in seconds. And increasingly we adopt this behaviour in work too. The role of marketing is often viewed as the most volatile. 'Sales are down! It's all marketing's fault!' or ' Sales are down, marketing, we need your help!' Whatever happens, marketing is increasingly put under stress to deliver. The business often can't live with us and can't live without us. And indeed, as mentioned in Chapter 3, it's one of the roles in the senior management team where you're most likely to get moved on first if progress isn't seen quickly.

It is therefore quite logical and very tempting to view all the activity that you undertake through the lens of this year and maybe next at most. Pressure internally to hit the lead targets for this month (or heaven forbid this week) or quarter can often mean that marketing's focus ends up leaning towards how to get the next click within your budget and make it convert over anything else. When you have an MD or CEO who is very focused on hitting all of the targets set each month or quarter at the expense of everything else, it does very often lead to a place of short-termism which often isn't good for the business.

In Chapter 5 I talked about the challenges around measuring marketing and this mindset of having to do all marketing by numbers – it doesn't help our short-term thinking. If we can't see the impact of an activity on a spreadsheet, then it makes it hard to justify its value, even if it's the right thing to do. The move to digital first marketing in the last few decades has brought incredible value to many businesses across the globe, there is no doubt, and helped to launch thousands of new travel businesses to the market. The downside to this is that marketing culture has changed to focus largely on what can be counted, not what has impact. And so, in an 'always on' world, our thinking becomes short-term too.

And this, I believe, is a trap. I have talked throughout the book about the increasing costs of digital marketing channels. The digital marketing landscape is dominated by a handful of global companies and the routes to reach our travellers are limited. This ultimately means that over time those channels become narrowed, competition increases and so does cost.

In all the events I've spoken at and attended post-Covid (and even pre-Covid, too), when the question of 'What is the one marketing activity that brings the most value?' is put to a panel of marketing directors or managers, the answer is nearly always 'Brand.' What they mean by this is that carrying out marketing activities that help to promote the travel company or their offering, rather than just pushing price or product, is often the best budget investment for the business. Brand marketing is something that every business should do more of, yet so many in travel don't. It's a big mistake to only focus on this quarter or this year, without thinking about a longer-term view or trying to build up some emotions within the target market for the future.

If you've been to any good marketing conference or follow any good marketing people on social media, then I would've hoped you'd have come across the oft-cited research by Binet and Field called 'The long and short of it'. It's one of the most famous pieces of marketing research and thinking this century so far and outlines the benefits of building a brand over the long term against just doing short-term tactics. They advocate for a balance of roughly 60 per cent of marketing budget on 'brand-building activity' (positioning your brand in the customers mind) against 40 per cent on 'sales activation' (short-term channels to generate sales now).[4] And while thirty years of research from nearly 1,000 marketing campaigns supports this view, a very large chunk of the travel world doesn't operate in this split at all.

In my humble opinion, I would say that perhaps most travel companies (at least ones with less than a £50 million turnover) operate in a 90 per cent/10 per cent split towards sales activation, with almost no concern about building brand. They are happy to operate in a world of Google Ads, Meta posts and weekly emails which bring in new leads and bookings but do little to help position the business for the long term. And while some of these activities do lead to awareness in the market and can be argued to help to build the brand, they are often transient formats and the message probably isn't positioning the brand in the target traveller's mind; it is very sales lead.

The other challenge is that if any budget or time is spent on any brand activities that don't have much obvious impact in the short term, often the business will decide that 'it wasn't worth it'. It was framed against more short-term activities in terms of measurability and didn't show much in the way of short-term uplift. For these and other reasons, the activity that had taken place gets written off and pressure builds again to go back to short-term activities.

To say it's a mistake to focus on the short term isn't necessarily true. We have to always get through the short term and create sales that give us the money in the bank to try to grow in the long term. Some travel businesses are still, many years on, recovering from the effects of the global pandemic and may well be for more years to come. In that environment, it makes sense to pull focus and budgets towards increasing sales in the next 12 months.

But, assuming that this isn't the case, then the mistake that most marketers and business owners make is failing to invest in the long term. Why do they not invest? I believe part of that reason is that they haven't completed a formal marketing education to make better decisions, or they have fallen into short-term activities which are too focused on next month's targets rather than next year's. Part of the problem is related to our HIPPOs, which I talked about in the previous section, where the pressure might be to lead with messaging focused on price, for example. Another large challenge is budget and finding ways to squeeze out some extra funds to spend on something that can help to build brand. How you answer these questions is up to you. But I would strongly recommend that you at least try. In a world where most marketing budgets are spent in the same way, most messaging is quite similar and most travel businesses lack the data to make better decisions, it would make a lot of sense to be different and go against the grain to find opportunities. The short-term thinking trap is a real one and in the next chapter we'll look more at how to broaden your thinking to try to stay ahead of the pack. For now, hold the thought of expanding your own thinking and planning to a longer term and how you can make that happen.

One client we worked with was looking to improve its digital marketing results. They had been with their previous PPC and data agency for several years but over time had become a bit stuck in a rut. Their performance hadn't grown and the final straw was the account manager who they liked to work with (despite the results) had recently left. They felt it was time for a change.

The client put out a brief to a number of agencies. We looked at their account and could find some quick wins to help improve their performance, and eventually won the client. Great news! And, sure enough, the changes we identified did have an impact. We saw sales go up, profitability increase, and in the first 12 months there was some good results shown which made the client feel positive and our team happy too.

But in the second year, as things went on, despite our team working as hard as ever and investing more time, the results started to taper off again. We looked at the Google Ads account, we looked at their analytics and we spoke to the client many times over many months. All of the metrics were still OK but sales weren't growing, and if anything were starting to decline. It wasn't until we reviewed some data from Google Trends that we realized that the brand searches had declined significantly in the time we had been working with them, and prior to that too. Our focus with PPC was to bring new people to the brand, rather than try to win over existing customers who already knew them. Brand traffic via PPC had declined slowly over 12 months but the overall interest in the brand had decreased significantly over a four or five year period.

After looking at every other option in our PPC toolset to try to improve performance, in our next meeting we had to bring up the matter of declining brand searches with the client, as the correlation between brand searches and overall effectiveness in their digital marketing was fairly strong. The marketing manager we spoke had only been in post a year or so (see the point made earlier in this chapter around marketing manager churn) and so they had to do more research internally as to why this might have been.

Why had the brand declined over time? What had changed?

The client had been spending a good chunk of their budget a decade ago sponsoring various events where their target market had been. They were seen at the right places, associated with other brands that were aligned to their target market and overall positioned the company in the right way for their audience. But this didn't deliver much in the way of short-term results. Having their name on banners or brochures didn't lead that audience to buy now.

But it did create awareness. It did create associations which weren't that obvious or measurable. When budgets tightened, the company had pulled out of some of the sponsorship deals that it had in the years previously. One by one, the company moved more and more of its budget to digital performance channels (i.e. PPC) and less into other areas. The positive hit of the month-by-month increase in sales via PPC was great in the first year or two. Lots of cheap website traffic (although much of it was brand related) leading to plenty of sales, all looking far cheaper than any other marketing activity. This all painted a picture of not needing to build brand, or if so, doing it in a cheaper way. The next year still showed good promise and justified the decision not to do so much brand spend from the previous year. That budget cut didn't make a difference at all!

By the time we were 18 months into working with the client and had unpicked the history of what they had been doing in the decade previously, the analysis was pretty stark. What was once a healthy, well-known and relevant brand had over time become too focused on the short-term wins without sticking with what had made it so aspirational in the first place. When potential buyers were looking around at where to spend their money, their first thought wasn't the brand, it was either rivals for their first port of call or, if unsure, the Google results pages.

But even then, without the brand work in the years before, in a list of search results, what good reason would there be to click on their advert over someone else's? The target buyer wouldn't know the brand and so would just click on the top few links and see if anything interested them. The decline in the awareness and aspiration of brand hadn't happened overnight, it'd happened over many years, just in the way it was built in the first place. A brand isn't built in a day, nor is it taken down as quickly. This client, though, had felt the impact of declined brand spend through the pain of going into the PPC auction against dozens of other companies and having to pay more per click each year, when only a few years earlier it was getting more clicks and a higher conversion rate due to the presence that it had. Very sadly, the marketing manager that we were working with struggled to tell this story (or rather their HIPPO didn't want to hear it). Obviously, when they spoke to other agencies about how to improve performance without this back story, they were sold a new dream of 'Come with us and it'll all be ok!' They left us, and within 12 months that marketing manager had left their role too.

This was one of the most real examples that I'd seen of the impact of a brand that was once well known, doing all of the right things but had made mistakes with their marketing over a number of years which ultimately led to the brand declining in size, credibility and ultimately success. Doing a Google Trends search today shows them at their lowest number on record and it would appear that in the years since we worked with them they have not been able to turn the tide. While this example looks at how things can go wrong when mistakes are made, it does also show how getting it right can counter these issues. The brand had invested in the right activities for several years before its peak, and when it was in its best days was able to attract customers outside of the search results pages, with revenue being generated directly without too much competition. This was achieved through activities like sponsorship and partnerships, as well as working hard with the trade to position them in a particular way. All of this was built over time but it led to good solid growth over a decade or more. Whether they had a 60/40 split on budget, it's impossible to know now. But investment was made and it paid back handsomely, just often years after the marketing budget was spent.

One thing we do know for sure is that by stopping that spend, the brand became less attractive and memorable and it cost more year on year to get the sales that they could, let alone back to the revenue numbers they were doing years before. If you're challenged on the reasons and cost of building a brand, perhaps it's worth sharing this story.

Summary

The ways that your marketing plans can go wrong are too many to list in this book – it could be a book in itself sadly. However, there are some key challenges that come up year after year that I believe are avoidable, and I've done my best here to explain what I see are the most common ones and how to overcome them.

Whether it's battling internal politics or managing HIPPOs, or believing the hype too much or taking on board too much content around the next big thing that's going to change the world in two years time, it's important to keep focused. There will of course be new challenges for any travel brands to navigate (see Chapter 1) but there will also be some core truths that will likely never change when it comes to travel. That rush of getting off a plane, that emotion that comes from meeting a new person in a new country, that experience that left its mark on your travellers which changed how they view the world – I believe these fundamental experiences help to make travel the best industry in the world to work in. How we get this message out to our potential audience though will always remain a challenge. As a digital marketer, it's very easy to make mistakes in your role or in your team. Having clarity about your target audience and keeping them always in your mind will help you stay on track and push back on things that aren't right for them. But this logic also applies to the digital marketing press as well as the travel one. Having a healthy curiosity and scepticism will help you slow down and make the right decisions in both the short and long term.

There are many things that we can learn from other mistakes, and I hope that I've helped you avoid some of the more common ones that I see others fall into.

Notes

1   Think Student. What is the average GCSE grade in the UK? Think Student, 2021. thinkstudent.co.uk/what-is-the-average- gcse -grade-in-the- uk / (archived at https://perma.cc/P3M3-M2GB)

2   Fortune. Amazon cuts hundreds of jobs in its Alexa unit as it doubles down on layoffs that already total more than 27,000 over the past year, Fortune, 2023. fortune.com/2023/11/17/amazon-layoffs-alexa-division-ai-andy-jassy/ (archived at https://perma.cc/DH6J-ZJL8)

3   Forbes. Bernard Arnault & family, Forbes, 2025. www.forbes.com/profile/ bernard-arnault/ (archived at https://perma.cc/4MYV-Y9UT)

4   A Murrell. Les Binet and Peter Field: The long and the short of it, Alex Murrell. 2024. www.alexmurrell.co.uk/summaries/les-binet-and-peter-field-the-long-and- the-short-of-it (archived at https://perma.cc/SY2T-PVLF)

7

How to keep ahead of the technology and travel trends

Introduction

In this final chapter we will look at the battle we all face as digital marketers – keeping abreast of technology and general travel trends. Weighing up the worth of moving towards new things that help not only us as marketers stay ahead, but also wider within our business offerings, is really important as travel businesses will face a lot of different challenges in the next few decades.

As mentioned throughout this book, digital media has changed why, how and where we travel, and has had an incredible impact on the travel industry. It has changed how our high streets look; it has changed the people that influence us and the way that we think about travel. And some of the changes in technology will continue to change things even further. The impact that digital technology has had on some travel companies has been extraordinary, either helping them to become some of the biggest in the sector or ultimately shutting their doors.

There are things that as digital marketers we need to be aware of in our roles and the businesses that we work in. From new digital apps that seemingly appear from nowhere to complete paradigm shifts in the way that we and the world operate, there will always be new opportunities and threats that pass our door. How we are influenced, where we feel safe to travel to, how much we can spend and the impact we leave on the world will all change and need to be thought about to keep us at the top of our game.

How can you keep ahead of these changes? What trends or changes might impact us and what things should you do to respond? I'll discuss these and other questions in this section, not to give direct answers, as sadly you'll need to do that yourself – the aim of this last chapter is to give you some ideas to go away and use as you need in the coming years ahead.

I will look at some of these things through lens of one of the most established frameworks in the business world, the PEST model. PEST stands for Political, Economic, Social and Technological and I'll look at some of the ways that they could change in the next decade or two. In the extended model of PESTLE, Legal and Environmental factors should also be considered. Our environment is crucial to how and where we travel; and the legal factors both at home and abroad can also have a huge impact on the world but particularly on technology, given the power that has built up in Silicon Valley.

Political

The changes to the world order will potentially have more impact than anything else that happens to your marketing plans. Threats of war, actual war or changes in leadership in certain countries have had marked impacts on where we travel in the 2020s more than perhaps any decade in recent memory. While we've had issues with certain areas and regions to contend with, ongoing international conflicts in the mid-2020s have changed tourism in many countries directly and others indirectly, too (it turns out that many people don't know where certain countries are in the world and sales can dip in countries not even remotely near to places of conflict). The pain and suffering for those in the countries of conflict is very real and far more of a concern than the impact of a travel business in the very grand scheme of things. While no one wants war for simple humanitarian reasons, from a travel business perspective it can have a catastrophic effect. I've worked with travel businesses that have seen longstanding destinations and product disappear from their websites overnight due to conflicts that have broken out. This has forced them to either shut or to quickly pivot into new products or locations to try to make up for the lost income and sales.

While no one truly knows that is going to happen in terms of conflicts in the coming years, it is safe to say that generally the world has become a lot more divided in political lines than in the recent past.

The old world order of politics is unlikely to come back in the next few decades, and the result could be that the countries that were once very safe turn out not to be in the not-too-distant future. What can you do about this? Well, ultimately nothing directly. However, for long-term planning it's worth looking at your key destinations and understanding more about the politics of both that country and the ones that surround it.

In your marketing role it's hugely important to keep abreast of the major news in your main destinations and their neighbours, as well as getting regular sentiment on the ground from local destination management companies (DMCs) if you can't do so yourself. Where you have multiple destinations that you serve, it becomes difficult to keep tabs on some or many destinations. The benefit of having multiple destinations to serve, of course, is that you will be much more spread in terms of risk. Should one or more of your countries face challenges both from a demand and delivery side of things, there are ways to offer alternatives to your audience or focus your marketing efforts on.

From a marketing perspective, it is always beneficial to be as close as possible to influential people or those in marketing roles within the destinations that you serve. From time to time, countries decide strategically at government level to push hard on tourism to help to put that country on the global map. Looking back at activity from countries in the Middle East since the turn of the century, we've seen clear investment from some of those governments to try to put themselves on the world map. The hosting of the World Cup in Qatar in 2022 was a very contentious announcement when it happened in 2010.

It was another indication of the ambition of the area to become a global power and use 'soft power' to get the country's name onto the lips of billions of people. And the ambition shown by Qatar is just one example of how the Arab states are determined to spend whatever it takes to bring the world to them, rather than anywhere else. While hosting a World Cup doesn't bring visitors and investment instantly, there are known residual effects of having events like this for years after and I fully expect there to be many more examples of this type of activity in the future.

The Line in Saudi Arabia is one such example: a 170km long enclosed city that will house up to nine million inhabitants by the time it is due to be completed in 2045.[1] It's a project that visually is like nothing else in the world and has ambition and scale that we've rarely ever seen. Whether the dream of The Line will ever be truly realized due to the completely eye-watering costs involved (anything from $300 billion up to $1 trillion by some recent estimates) remains to be seen, but there will no doubt be something of some scale to show the world in the next decade. And if it's even half as good as it looks on the artist impressions and models, it will be a place people will want to visit, stay and perhaps even live as the region continues to create places of aspiration which so very few countries are able to achieve. How this changes tourism, the view of the region as a place to visit or even live is something to watch. If, and it is a very big if given the scale of the project, it gets near what is set out, then it could certainly change a lot of travel and tourism from where we are today.

And where people live is probably the final big trend to spend time thinking about in your marketing role. I've talked here about the changes that are happening around the world in terms of wars and changing political powers and alignments. One of the biggest factors influencing voting patterns and how some view the world is immigration. In the UK it has changed our politics markedly since 2000, and the same is true in many European countries. While the growth in immigration has not been tackled properly in recent times, I suspect it will continue to either get worse or flatline in the next decade or two. Whatever happens to the actual numbers, it will continue to be a factor when it comes to where the general public vote.

Where people want to live and can actually live across the globe is going to change hugely according to various factors, mostly environmental. Up to three billion people are expected to move around the planet by 2100.[2] While a large percentage of these people will live in Asia and Africa, the effect of migration and hospitable living conditions is going to change significantly. This is going to bring many changes for most governments around the world, either directly or indirectly. They will have to handle changes to the physical environment of their countries but also the flow of people to and from it. How much of an impact this is going to have in the time of you reading this and it then having a direct effect on how and where you market is, is unknown. If anyone knew then they would be doing something about it! How high up you put this on your list of things to think about (when there is plenty to be getting on with already!) will depend on how far ahead you are thinking as a business and with your marketing plans. If you are taking a long-term view over the next five years of building a brand and expertise in a destination when it potentially faces significant political, economic and immigration challenges will not be easy. How the political leaders handle those challenges within the countries that you work closely with will be worth taking time to truly understand, as it could change both the specific places that you can send travellers to or their perceptions of that place.

Economic

In the last few decades, the tectonic plates of the global economy have shifted markedly. China, which at the end of the 20th century was outside the top 10 of global economies, is now perhaps the biggest economy in the world and certainly shows no sign of shrinking, while other countries have started to stagnate following the 2008 financial crisis. China continues to invest and lead the world in all sorts of areas, like solar, electric vehicle (EV) technology and AI, which should help it to continue to fuel its place as the biggest economy globally. Huge investment in infrastructure projects has also pushed many countries in the Middle East to attract continued investment and growing gross domestic product (GDP) figures. You'll no doubt have seen pictures of countries like Saudi Arabia or Dubai which in the mid-1900s were mostly deserts with a few large buildings scattered around the cities. The transformation in the capital cities of the modern Middle East is barely believable.

These new global powers have growing economies which have brought in new investments and residents. Why? Because Western worlds and governments haven't managed to achieve or sustain growth that they have historically. Growth predictions in the UK in spring 2025 were around 1.5 per cent for the next five years, with inflation still lurking in the background higher than anyone would like.[3] The same is expected around a lot of Europe. And with Covid only just out of the rear-view mirror, many governments are now carrying more debt than ever before, with interest payments making up more and more of the overall spend each year. Each government has less room to invest in areas which will pay back in the long term as well and struggle to get the growth that they need or want to get through the next election cycle. It's not to say that that times are hard. While more countries than ever before have higher living standards than at any other point in their history, it doesn't translate to the lived experience for many, leading to increased dissatisfaction.

With growth fairly flat, investment flat and wages also fairly flat, what does this mean for the general outlook in the Western world and what is the impact on travel? As we'll look at later, perhaps these things are great for travel! More people have more reasons to go on holiday (both positive and negative) and it opens up many opportunities for the whole travel industry to capture new and different travellers.

However, the reality is that when stagnation hits economies, household budgets will generally start to get squeezed. The average salary in the UK in 2025 is around £31,600,[4] typical rent costs are around £1,300 per month[5] and interest/mortgages are now at the highest they have been for over a decade, with the result being that people generally have less disposable income.

Holidays and travel are, and probably always will be, high priorities for people. But when finances are tight, our choices reduce, and we end up going for the cheapest or perhaps 'best value' options that we can. Research from ATOL shows that in 2019 the top 10 holders of licences in the UK made up 65 per cent of the overall capacity. In 2025, that number was at 82 per cent.[6] More people are travelling with more mass market carriers who can keep their prices lower due to increases in volumes, and so it goes on. In much the same way technology has concentrated money and profit into a handful of companies, in travel in the UK the same is broadly true. This is only possible when the economy creates the conditions for this to happen. If the economy had more growth, then more people would have more disposable income, which would in turn diversify the choices that consumers make.

What could this mean for you and how do you get ahead of this?

If you offer mid-market or luxury travel options, then there is a strong chance that your available audience may shrink in the coming years in a market that creates less wealth and opportunity. This may mean having to change your focus (back to Chapter 2) from who you currently focus on, to new age groups, demographics or geographies. Alternatively, you may have to think about your price points and/or how you package your itineraries. Could you take certain parts of your offering out? Or allow travellers to buy less – e.g. instead of seven days defaults, perhaps four days becomes an option to get the same experience at a lower price point. Perhaps you can focus on 'newer' destinations which offer similar experiences and comparable facilities or weather but are cheaper? Perhaps you can price certain packages at the lower end of an ideal average booking value to get more interest but then work harder to do upsells pre-trip to bring in additional income.

There are many ways that you can break down your pricing or product so that you make it within reach of more people while staying aspirational and not damaging how your audience might perceive your brand. In terms of how you stay ahead of these buying trends, there is no one answer. What you might think is important to one group of people, like home ownership historically has been, is, for the younger generation, not something that they aspire to as much. When the likelihood of ever being able to buy a property seems completely beyond reach, aspirations and priorities can change quite dramatically. To think ahead, particularly when it comes to the money in your travellers' pockets, as with a lot of things mentioned throughout the book, keeping a regular eye on the things that affect their world and having a good picture of their needs and wants is key. If you are targeting a younger age group, then they will be much more likely to be price sensitive than, say, a company targeting affluent retirees. Being aware of the financial pressures that your specific audience face and how that changes over time is hugely important, so reading updates from banks, financial institutions or travel experts who also understand markets is very useful.

Travellers may lead different lifestyles and have different expectations, but they all want to purchase a good product. They will always be seeking value, doing their best to make their budget go as far as they can and trying to get the best trip with the most reputable brand that they can. Just because a trip is cheap it doesn't mean it's poor, and just because a trip is expensive doesn't mean that it's going to be great. With an almost infinite number of facts, opinions and reviews at their fingertips, travellers are perhaps now savvier than ever and will spot a bad deal when they see one.

The final thing to be aware of, particularly if your travel business deals with a lot of overseas suppliers, is the exchange rates between your head office(s) and the places where you travel to. The cost of flights particularly can have a very big impact on the desirability and aspiration of where your travellers end up going. In the 2020s, the cost of flights to some longer haul destinations has increased markedly (up to 15 per cent in one year when the European energy crisis started in 2022),[7] and if this were to carry on in the future then it is going to affect your ability to sell and the audiences that you can realistically target.

Additionally, just what your travellers can buy with the left-over money that they have while they are away (unless you are offering all-inclusive packages) is going to have an impact. This can work both ways, though, so if you're seeing favourable rates to the destinations that you're taking your travellers to from your source markets, then this can be a great opportunity to push harder on sales messages, while things swinging the other way may lead to lower numbers of passengers.

One example of economic factors having a big impact on the UK market was post-Brexit when the value of the pound dropped markedly against the US dollar and the euro, which led to a temporary increase in visitors for the summer of 2016 when suddenly it was a lot cheaper to visit and spend in the UK.[8] Exchange rates are linked to political changes, which are important to keep an eye on, along with the other factors outlined in this section. In this simple Brexit example, a big 'moment' such as a vote or election can have a substantial impact on demand both ways and it's worth being aware of this for not only your primary countries where you travel to, but also those around them where there is a potential knock-on effect.

Social

The grouping of generations into buckets is a relatively new thing in the marketing, and now, sadly, wider world. The term 'millennial' has been thrown around so much in recent times to render it almost useless. Additionally, plenty of people smarter than me have taken a lot of effort to highlight the futility of trying to stereotype millions of people just by the year they were born. Just because someone happened to be born in the same arbitrary time period eight years after me doesn't mean I have anything more in common with them compared to someone in another group born eight years earlier. The way we each live our lives is influenced by hundreds of factors, many of which are bigger and more important than the year that we are born in.

While there are occasionally some benefits to be found in looking at trends by decades or arbitrary groupings of people, the bigger benefit comes from published research looking at age, technology and psychographics, which are more likely to have direct impacts on our travel business and who we sell our trips to.

Let's look first at age demographics in the UK. Our population, like most Western world countries, is ageing up, not down. The *Guardian* highlighted several years ago how the older population is living longer as time goes on.[9] Increasingly, science is finding new ways to keep people living longer, which is great for us as individuals but as a wider society creates challenges.

The number of people in the UK over the age of 65 is going to increase hugely in the 2030s, and will no doubt grow further as time goes on. The same trend is happening in the US, where it is predicted that in 2034 there will be more people over 65 than under 18 for the first time in US history.[10]

This trending up of age in society is going to create further divides between generations, both politically well as economic. Governments will have to battle to deal with more people becoming less productive and relying on the state in many ways, as well as differing world views bringing different priorities on policy. While governments battle with that, the wealth gap between generations is likely to grow too.

The cost of housing in the Western world has largely followed the other trends where overall things tend to favour the older generations. Getting on the housing ladder has become increasingly difficult for the younger generations with the gap between median salary and house prices growing by over 300 per cent since the year 2000. In its simplest terms, this means it's now three times harder to get on the properly ladder now than it was in the past.[11] While each government has promised to build more homes at each election, the reality to date at least, has been incredible under-performance when it comes to hitting the new build targets. Research carried out by Channel 4 back in 2017 suggested that various governments in the UK had under-delivered on home build targets by 600,000 homes[12] and it's not got any better since. Given the performance of all governments in the last few decades, it would be highly unusual if this trend reversed in the years ahead. The net effect will be fewer of the next generation owning homes without even more help from their parents or grandparents, including passing homes or assets down to younger generations.

What could this mean for travel and you? There are several ways to look at it. Firstly, if people are living longer and have value in their houses, it is likely that they will have more disposable income either through having pensions and no mortgages to spend on trips, or through releasing value by selling their property and downsizing to free up funds.

For younger generations, if the task of saving hard to go on to own a property is simply too big, then they potentially won't even start and will instead rent or stay at home for longer. The percentage of families in England with adult children living with their parents increased by 14 per cent from 2011 to 2021, showing growth in nearly every age group apart from 16- and 17-year-olds.[13] The 'ageing up' of households and families perhaps gives the opportunity for those selling family holiday trips to increase the age of the target audience (or perhaps the inverse is true – do you want to holiday together when you live together full time?).

For those younger people who live at home with their parents, their rent (if any) will be far cheaper than going to private landlords, giving them more disposable income. And with phone usage the highest in younger audiences, they can be inspired by social videos and friends, and so be more inclined to travel more than previous generations of the same age. A survey carried out by McKinsey in 2024 showed that those between 18 to 25 showed a greater interest in travel than any other age group, which gives opportunities to those catering to younger groups to still grow and entice travellers, perhaps albeit it with lower budgets.[14]

Either way you slice it, it would appear that the appetite and ability to travel for all age groups should only increase, particularly at the younger and older ends of the market.

The question, then, is how these groups will prefer to travel. With environmental changes afoot (see section later), the choice that travellers make will again pose opportunities and threats to travel businesses. The awareness of the impact we have on the world, or perhaps the importance of this in terms of choices we make, again varies by generation.

In research produced by Kantar in 2025, the percentage of people who felt bad about the environmental impact of travel went from 35 per cent in young people to just 18 per cent for those over 65.[15] Depending on who you're selling travel to will dictate how much time and effort you will need to spend (or not) highlighting your environmental credentials. These differences in views between generations don't tend to present themselves hugely in the mainstream but they are there and need to be considered in both your marketing but also your actual product. It is worth bearing in mind that the actual gap between the two needs to be understood. While your product might have less impact overall as time goes on, that doesn't necessarily mean that your travellers will want to spend more on it. The 'do/say' gap has been fairly consistent over time in travel, where travellers will say that they want 'better' travel products which have less impact on the planet. Sadly, the reality is that travellers don't spend as much on these experiences as they say.

Exodus Travels, a B Corp company based in the UK, asked what was the most important factor when booking a holiday in a survey carried out in 2025. Of the 15 options available, 'lower environmental impact' came out 13th on the list (with quality of itinerary and tour leader knowledge coming out top and second respectively). Even among those who have travelled with companies known for having better overall societal and environmental credentials, the importance of these factors still isn't as big as it is purported to be.

Does this mean that, as time goes on, the 'green factor' starts to diminish? Personally, I hope not, and don't expect it to. Should some of the environmental problems grow around weather and nature as predicted, then it's going to make *how* we travel as much of an issue as where in the minds of large groups of people across all ages. The societal pressures to 'do the right thing' should increase as time goes on, yet how this manifests itself in terms of traveller choices and spend is one to watch.

The final societal factor that I believe is going to be incredibly important in the years ahead is trust. Trust both in terms of backing up what you deliver and how you act with your current travellers, and reflecting that online in all of your digital touchpoints. The large OTAs like Booking.com have talked at many travel conferences about how fraud now pervades their platforms and that they have to intercept 50 million malicious links a month. This number is only going to increase as time goes on.[16]

The power of AI to create hyper-realistic images, videos and personalized messages is well known. How this will impact the way we view brands, destinations and the world around us as time goes on is unknown. However, there is no turning back.

Anecdotally, I've spoken to many people in the last few years about how untrustworthy certain parts of the internet are and how they now start in a place of distrust with what they see online rather than one of trust by default. How we experience the internet, social media, online video and interact with our devices is already very subjective as we all behave in different ways and share different data. And the bubbles we live in online will potentially only get bigger and more confused as what we see reflected back at us becomes more specific and personalized.

I've absolutely no doubt that trust when it comes to brands and travel is going to be even more important than it is now. As a marketer, the more you can build your reputation with trusted businesses and organizations to show the world that you are real and authentic will become crucial. If there are chances to verify your company in certain platforms, then you should take them. If you can build your brand in trusted websites and publications then this is again something you should do, alongside your other digital channels.

As time goes on, your audience will become more savvy and more aware of the 'fakeness' that goes on within the internet, not only from brands trying too hard to create false impressions of their trips, but also from copy-cat fraudsters who try to look like you or your competitors. While your business might be lucky and dodge 'copycatting', your competitors might not, and some residual effect might still pass across to you. I have no doubt that in the future on the internet it will become so hard to tell truth from falsehood that society will change as a result. Convincing our current and potential travellers that we are real and trustworthy might, in time, become one of marketing's biggest challenges of all.

Technological

During the time of writing this book, the AI hype train has showed absolutely no sign of slowing down. What started many years ago in the background, firstly with Google's acquisition of Deepmind (a UK-based AI company) back in 2014[17] and their subsequent use of this AI technology through both SEO and PPC, in later years, through to the explosive growth of ChatGPT released nearly a decade later, the talk of AI in digital marketing is seemingly all-pervasive.

Looking back to some of the headlines I referenced in Chapter 1 about how the internet was once described, it's very easy to make the comparison between then and now. Where once there were headlines in every paper about the hype and promise of the internet, we seem to be back at the same place roughly three decades later. Back in the late 1990s the hype and expectation grew to such an unmanageable level that many companies went bust and many investors pulled out of the market, resulting the dot-com bubble popping in 2000, with many stocks failing and some, like Cisco, losing 80 per cent of their value.[18]

In the mid-2020s, the hype and hysteria around AI is just as prevalent. 'AI is going to transform travel forever!', 'If you don't shift your entire travel business to be AI first in the next 12 months you'll go out of business' are the types of headline I read on a weekly basis. There are many travel companies in start-up mode that want this change to happen, but whether it will or not remains to be seen.

What is indisputable, though, is that Silicon Valley is betting insane amounts of money that AI will help them to continue their growth and dominance. In 2024, an estimated $175 *billion* dollars was spent on cloud computing infrastructure by just *four* companies, as shown in Figure 7.1, with billions of dollars also spent by other 'smaller' ones. If the biggest companies in the world are putting in tens of billions of dollars each, then they are going to need to get returns back on their investments. For some of them, they see this as essential to their very existence. Don't invest, and in less than a decade they could be much, much smaller than they are now. Push to be part of the game and they can at least defend their position in the market or push on an increase in revenue and profits further. The changes brought about by AI and the impact that it will have on both digital marketing and operations in travel remain to be seen and if I knew what they were, then I wouldn't be writing this book!

At this point, search engines still rule the roost, with travellers with the total number of searches conducted on Google being 373 times more than ChatGPT.[19] However, Google sees opportunity in AI interfaces, with AI Overviews (AIOs) being fully rolled out in 2025 to the mainstream in all main markets. This change to the search engine results pages (SERPs) is the next step on from 'Featured Snippets', which first started to appear in 2021.[20] AIO is the next step in Google controlling the user experience and giving more real estate to its own answers, rather than sending users off into the internet to get what they want. Given this is how all LLMs like Claude, Perplexity, ChatGPT and others operate, and are their biggest threats, it seems foolish to assume that Google will go back to a more diverse interface.

FIGURE 7.1 The growth in spending on cloud platform infrastructure by Meta, Alphabet (Google), AWS (Amazon) and Microsoft

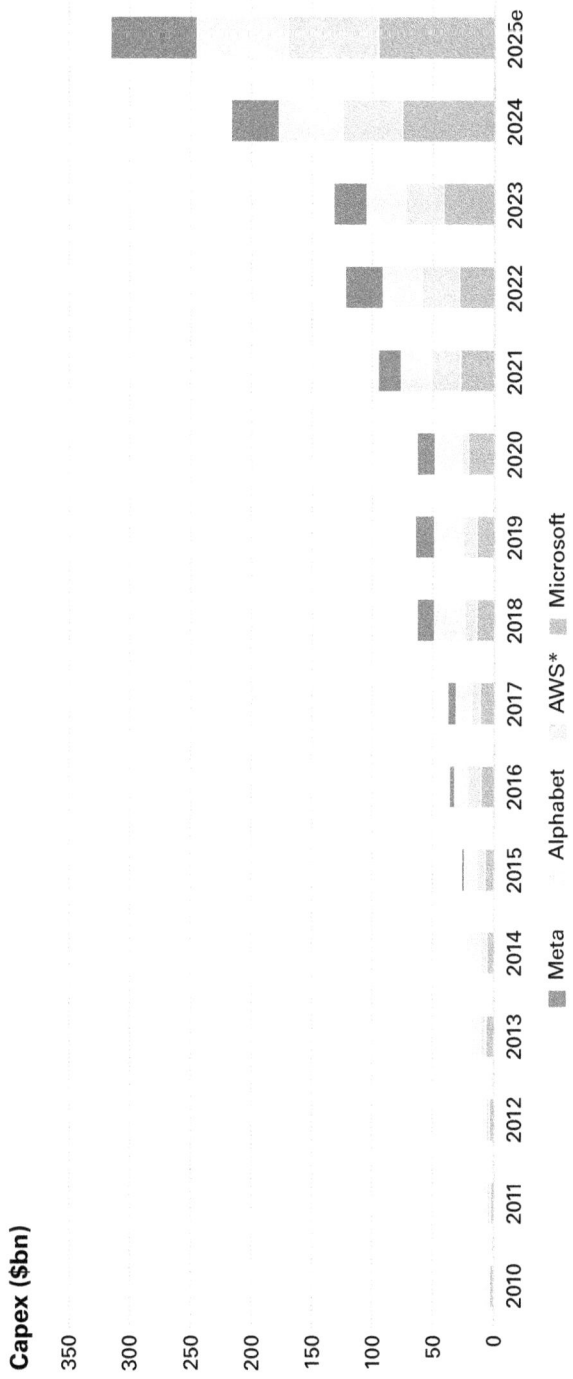

Capex ($bn)

Legend: Meta, Alphabet, AWS*, Microsoft

SOURCE Courtesy of Benedict Evans (2025)

And with more control over the results shown to users, the more influence Google can have over how and where users click. In a 2024 study by long-time digital marketing stalwart Rand Fishkin and his team at Sparktoro, they highlighted that nearly 2 in 3 clicks stay in the Google ecosystem.[21] Rand and his team also did research back in 2018 which showed that the number of clicks on PPC ads had grown from 1.5 per cent in 2016 to 3.4 per cent in less than three years, an increase of 230 per cent.[22]

Whist we don't have any data since then to follow this trend in PPC clicks, what we do know is with more control over the search results page and more of its own content being shown, Google is going to send less traffic in the future. Google's aim will be to create more value in the clicks out to websites, which I expect will only result in more costs to us as marketers. The days of getting free clicks to our website are on the slow decline and the future will be more about letting the algorithms (in whatever flavour) doing their thing on our behalf with very little control.

Google's release of Performance Max ad campaigns in late 2021 meant 'basically PPC is over' according to one industry veteran I spoke to at the time, due to the way it distributed ads across the Google network without giving advertisers any real control. Google's reason for releasing Pmax was to help advertisers 'save them time' but in the process took away a huge amount of control that had been there in the years before. Pmax has often turned out not to save any time at all, as many marketers have chosen not to use it as it has often wasted budgets or generated large amounts of poor-quality leads.[23] That hasn't stopped Google, though, and with the introduction of AI Max in 2025 Google has pushed again to take away further control from advertisers, not only presenting ads in Google where it wants but also creating ad assets by itself, again with limited human effort or input.

This automatic approach to search and display marketing by Google, combined with an ever-tightening grip on the results pages, will only mean less control and influence over search campaigns for us as marketers from this point onwards. We can fight back with better data signals, as mentioned in Chapter 5, but our options to influence results are becoming limited. Meta is second only to Google when it comes to advertising budgets spent globally and is used by thousands of travel companies across the world. When its owner Mark Zuckerberg said publicly in 2025 that he wants to 'fully automate advertising on Meta by 2026'[24] he wasn't hiding his ambition to take complete control of every aspect of how ads run in his world.

Wherever we look, the black boxes running our digital advertising are getting bigger, more opaque and harder to control. We will be in a world very soon where the messaging and creative used to sell our brand will be out of our control and in the hands of the biggest companies in the world.

How can we possibly win in this type of world?

> The big focus for me is to go back to the principles set out in Chapter 2. Think about your overall marketing strategy. Who are you serving? What makes you different? Why should travellers take the time to view your ad, let alone make an enquiry? If it's just price, then you're probably in a losing battle. If you don't have enough differentiation in your brand against competitors, then the algorithm is less likely to pick you from dozens or hundreds of others. Creating bold and distinctive assets has always been important but will become even more so. Start investing now in the best video, imagery and words that can bring your trips and experiences to life. These, alongside high-quality data, are likely to bring you the best success as the machines start to take over more and more.

Outside of digital marketing, what other technologies should we be aware of?

Many new types of technology have been touted in the last decade which haven't really changed mainstream behaviours: crypto, blockchain, virtual reality and augmented reality, non-fungible tokens (NFTs), 3D printing… They have been seen as the 'next big thing' at one point or another and then disappeared into the background. These technologies have all got a place somewhere in the world, but I would be very surprised if any of them had any impact on what you do.

The exception here could be augmented reality (AR) technology, which continues to drop in price and increases in quality. By having a computer in a pair of glasses, more opportunities open up for travel to offer in destination experiences as well as offering real-time translation either on screen or linked up with headphones (as is possible now). By offering up the ability to see around your world with additional content, exclusive offers and having almost no translation issues (e.g. menus/guidance, etc.), travellers will be able to remove some of the final barriers that perhaps stop them travelling to more far away places where language and navigation add excessive friction.

Will AR glasses or similar (contact lens have long been prototyped) hit the mainstream? It feels a stretch as several people I know who like and advocate for new tech still see them as 'toys' – but it could be possible. A big factor stopping mass adoption, even after a decade of AR glasses being available in some guise, is security and privacy. When we are near people with 'always on cameras' on their faces it can cause many more issues than are solved for the individual. Is the ability to take a photo at any point worth it when anyone who is near us behaves very differently through fear of being watched and analysed?

If they do become popular, will this add to the travel experience or just keep travellers more in their 'own' world? Who knows. But for us as marketers, having travellers travel with some major friction points being removed certainly opens up some more opportunities.

Legal

The concentration of powers that I've seen accumulated in the big tech world has been both interesting and scary to watch during my career. From scrappy start-ups to influencing elections, world orders and society, it's been rare in history to have such vast wealth and power located in so few hands. During times in recent history, we've experienced situations where too much power accumulated in too few places, but in those times elected officials tended to do something about it.

From the breaking up of Standard Oil over 100 years ago in the US (where 90 per cent of all oil production was with one company), AT&T in the 1980s which was broken up into many smaller business (to prevent them having too much control in the telecommunications world), through to Microsoft being told that they couldn't bundle Internet Explorer with Windows in the late 1990s (opening the way for Google to grow), when governments have had to intervene to create new opportunities for competition and prevent monopolies from being created or run, they've done so.

With Google effectively having a monopoly in a lot of the Western world for a decade or more, Meta owning three of the biggest social apps globally and Amazon controlling the vast majority of ecommerce in the US and other countries, there are many places where splitting up companies would make huge sense in the long-term interests of economies and for consumers.

The EU has been reasonably pushy in the last decade with US big tech companies, fining them on multiple occasions for breaking various privacy rules. But both they and the US courts haven't been able to make much headway regarding the structure of these companies. That tide does seem to be changing though.

In 2024, Judge Amit Mehta (I do like the ironic name of the judge) ruled that Google had acted as monopolist and so violated Section 2 of the Sherman

Act (as US anti-competitive law).[25] The result was that the Department of Justice bought a case against Google outlining their monopolistic deals, with various companies like Apple, which effectively locked users into their search engine for many years, to the detriment of others. At this time the case is still going on but one of the potential outcomes could be that something like Chrome or possibly Android will be divested from the company. And if the court ruling is a success, there is a chance that other companies might be targeted in a similar way. Instagram as a stand alone, Apple's App store being run by a separate company or AWS being spun out of Amazon are all some things that could happen.

What would be the impact on you directly? The biggest ones to keep an eye on here are Google and Meta and if they get broken up. If they are then this could impact on how users find their way through the internet and to your websites potentially. It could also impact your data collection and analysis with potentially more channels to collect from (or not) and analyse.

> We can't influence how governments around the world will regulate or change things. The control that these companies have is almost beyond imagination, and with that comes huge influence in the halls of power. This isn't by accident. Meta, Google, Amazon and other tech companies are now the biggest spenders when it comes to lobbying in Washington and Brussels.[26] Taking action is hard. If things do change, then you'll be in the same boat as every other marketer across the globe. But it's important to be ready. Keep tabs on the news around technology court cases as they come up. While it's been my want for a long time that something would be done, it's now my belief that something will change as things can't stay as they are. Power, money and influence are only getting stronger in the world of big tech, and sooner or later the prospect of not doing something will be too damaging. Being a first mover in whatever change might happen is only ever going to be beneficial, so while there is nothing to be done now, being aware of things can only be helpful.

It could well be years before things change in big tech. However, pressures in local cities and towns around the world where tourism is a large part of the economy and having a detrimental impact on residents will make action happen faster. Prior to Covid, many of the conferences I attended talked at length about over-tourism and how some places around the world were at breaking point. The lockdowns obviously reset that but, in the years, since the problem in some places has got even worse. And some cities and countries are using many legal powers to try to push back on tourism where possible or support local citizens so that they don't get squeezed out. Mass tourist hot spots like Venice and Barcelona have passed multiple laws and legislation to favour locals to try to stem the people and money coming into the cities by introducing taxes, restrictions and other measures wherever possible. As part of travel becomes fuelled by algorithms and more people decide that they want to tick another place off their bucket lists, it's fair to assume that more and more famous destinations are going to get more and more busy. The likelihood of what we've already started to see with tourism taxes (which have to this point been additional tax income rather than any deterrent), property restrictions and the like are likely to get more severe and widespread. I'd argue that this is a great thing overall as there are so many inspirational places scattered across the globe and hidden gems waiting to be found. The more travel is spread out across cities and countries the better, although if you are selling to the mass market and 'tourist hot spots' then obviously this isn't going to help you in the short term.

> Get close to destination management companies in your key areas to understand any possible changes that might be happening in your major locations. They should know before anyone else about any possible laws or legislation that might be coming down the line or any issues that are happening on the ground that haven't been reported in the press. Also seek out any tourism newsletters or social channels/personalities that cover issues on the ground so that you can get additional sources of information concerning your areas of interest.

Environmental

You don't need me to tell you that we have an ongoing challenge which is going to affect every single person on earth in the coming decades – global climate breakdown. We can't call it global warming as for some places changes in climate will not result in warmer temperatures, but the opposite. And I personally prefer the word breakdown as this is fundamentally what it is. It is change, but change often implies progress. The warming of the planet isn't. The increases in global temperature are not slowing down and, if anything, are starting to creep up each and every year.

This is perhaps the biggest issue facing the globe in the coming decades and the one that could potentially change your travel business forever. If you can't reliably take your guests on the trips that you have created, then what business do you have? You either shut your doors or you shift focus to other products or locations. Both are potentially viable options although with very different outcomes. The fact that world temperatures, weather and climate are fundamentally changing now and will continue to do so from this point onwards is frankly discussed criminally infrequently. It's the one gigantic elephant in the room which I think continues to sit there as business and political leaders continue to ignore it, not wanting to be the bearer of bad news in terms of the reality of the situation.

In all of the dozens of conferences I've attended in my time in the travel industry, it's a topic that has only come up a few times and there have been scant few speakers on it either. We don't want to really hear about the destruction that is happening around the globe unless there are greater powers than us that are on hand to share a soundbite without much in the way of accountability. The peak of interest around Blue Planet Two in 2017 was a high point for environmental awareness in many parts of the world but to my mind hasn't happened since. There was a moment where it felt like change for the better would happen and that there was enough willing to really put some positive change into action. Sadly, since then, wild fires, droughts and flash floods have become part of the news cycle and we've all become fairly apathetic to what's happening. I know I have. Climate break-down isn't a one-off event, it's life. And so the impact on you or your marketing challenges probably might not happen this year. Or next. But it will at some point and you need to be ready.

Figure 7.2 visualizes the challenge ahead. The UK's Met Office produced this graph which highlights the changes in global surface temperature since the turn of the century. And you will have no doubt seen the temperature stripes graphics first created by Professor Ed Hawkins at Reading University and used by dozens of organizations, including Greenpeace. There are many ways to show the increases in temperature, but however you see it, the graphs don't look great.

What's the impact of this on your travel business? Well, as with any good question, the answer is 'It depends.' While some counties and cities are seemingly getting only minor changes in climate, some are seeing some larger changes. Ongoing wildfires, droughts, heat warnings, flash floods or stark swings in temperature are happening all around the world to varying degrees.

The impact on your travel business could be fairly large and fairly soon. In the 'State of travel' report published by Skift in 2024,[27] they highlighted that extreme weather events is the third highest ranked challenge for international travel identified by their panel.

FIGURE 7.2 Global average surface temperature since 2000

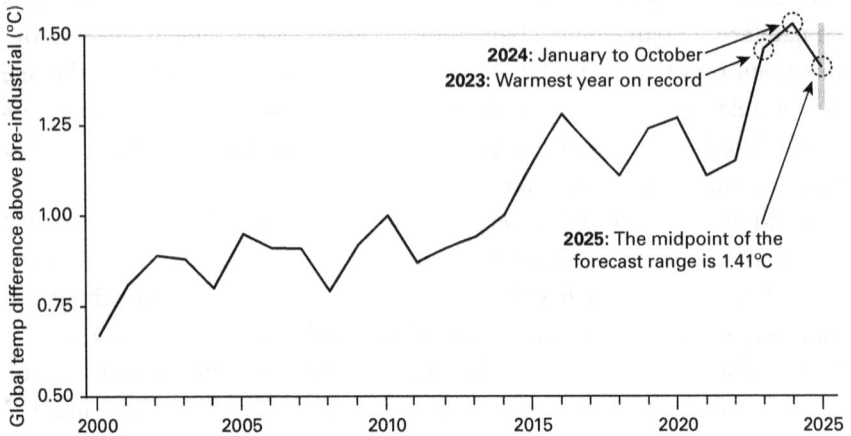

SOURCE Courtesy of The Met Office. Contains public sector information licensed under the Open Government Licence v3.0

Countries like Spain, Greece and Cyprus were for decades the mainstays of travel to/from the UK but they have started to get affected by temperatures being too high in peak months. If your travel business specializes in these locations, then the mid- and long-term outlook could perhaps be less than favourable. It might be worthwhile looking now at expanding your 'season' to include shoulder months such as March or October where possible, as travellers seek to travel when temperatures are milder or less extreme. While some operators perhaps face challenges ahead, for others, opportunities for growth appear. The word 'coolation' has been used in recent times to describe the trend for some travellers to go abroad to new countries which have less extreme heat in peak travel months.

I've no doubt that the travel industry will find a way to smash two words together in the coming years to describe further changes in travel tastes based on climate changes around the globe. If we keep on with our current emission levels and temperature charts in the next decade or two, various scenarios could play out, and frankly none of them look great. Quite how we prevent this happening is not within the bounds of this book. If we assume that governments around the world don't act fast enough and the world suffers as a result (see the 'Political' section above) then there will be huge changes in how, where and when we travel in the future.

The power to change how climate affects any of us is tiny. While we can all do our own thing personally and within our businesses to reduce our carbon footprint and waste, there are going to be limits to what we can achieve. If we can look at ourselves in the mirror and within our teams and know that we're doing as much as we can then that is our first start.

How anyone can keep ahead of the changes that are going to impact us is impossible to say. The environmental factors and changes that your travel business is going to see could well be minimal, which would be great for business and open up lots of opportunities. If your products and destinations are going to be reasonably unaffected, that is something to very much outline in your communications. Should that happen, then you could also expect to see increases in demand as travellers move away from more traditional destinations. This could be a huge opportunity and one that should be monitored from afar periodically. Put it on your marketing meeting agendas each quarter or annual reviews to ensure that you're monitoring the trends that happen in your key locations. Data is available to track this from trusted sources like the Met Office or Climate.gov which can help give factual data on the places most important to you without any bias applied.

It's worth ending with the stark fact that no one truly knows what is going to happen in the next decade or beyond. The temperatures of the planet haven't been this high for millennia and are on a growth rather than decline curve. Even if we can radically reduce our carbon output it will still be too late to go back to how things were in the recent past.

The change has been cast and so it's then about how we adopt. One of our biggest challenges outside the destinations we go to and trips we offer will be how we communicate the impact the changing climate has on our locations. We need to reassure our travellers that their money is safe with us and say how our business is responding to limit your impact on the globe.

Summary

Throughout these sections I've tried to highlight just some of the wide variety of trends that are occurring across the world right now. Technology is obviously going to have a big impact on how we, as digital marketers, operate and find new clients. With that said, we can't just focus on technology alone. Digital channels allow us to find, interact with and win new travellers. But the world of digital is just a version of the real world and reflects what is happening outside of it too.

Politics, the economy, environmental and societal shifts can and will impact who you market to and the successes that you will achieve in your role. All of these factors and some others will have to be thought about to some degree. The changes that I've seen in my 20+ year career in terms of how and where we travel have been stark. None of them happened overnight but, if you look back at certain points in history, you can see where they started.

How you apply all of these thoughts to your own role and the business you work at now will be down to you. Only you know the products that you offer, the audience that you want to target, your competitors, the locations you go to and how your market works. The aim of this chapter is to widen your thinking about what it takes to think long-term and strategically about how you can take your marketing up a level in the future. How that pans out is up to you. What I do know is that doing what you're doing now is not going to work in five years' time. There are many things going on in the world that will change the shape of your role and career. If you can keep a wide view by reading, listening to and watching experts in their fields, you will build up a much richer understanding of the changes going on. You will be able to be ahead of your competition as well as adding a lot more value to your business and team. So few marketers go above and beyond in their roles or have a knowledge of the world that affect them and their business, and if you can start to think about some of the areas highlighted here, you'll be that much better prepared than everyone else.

Notes

1 Neom. The Line, Neom. www.neom.com/en-us/regions/theline (archived at https://perma.cc/X4H3-J462)

2 G Vince. Is the world ready for mass migration due to climate change? BBC, 2022. www.bbc.co.uk/future/article/20221117-how-borders-might-change-to-cope-with-climate-migration (archived at https://perma.cc/C74J-WUND)

3 Office for Budget Responsibility. Economic and fiscal outlook March 2025, Office for Budget Responsibility, 2025. obr.uk/docs/dlm_uploads/OBR_Economic_and_fiscal_outlook_March_2025.pdf (archived at https://perma.cc/U4FS-4TPE)

4 S Samson. What is the average UK Salary? Complete guide to UK earnings in 2025, Resume Kraft, 2025. resumekraft.com/average-uk-salary/ (archived at https://perma.cc/4HYE-ELML)

5 Office for National Statistics. Private rent and house prices UK: June 2025, ONS, 2025. www.ons.gov.uk/economy/inflationandpriceindices/bulletins/privaterentandhousepricesuk/june2025 (archived at https://perma.cc/ULB9-6SNN)

6 Travel Trade Consultancy. The biggest trends in the March 2025 ATOL authorisation data, Travel Trade Consultancy, 2025. traveltradeconsultancy.co.uk/news-insights/the-biggest-trends-in-the-march-2025-atol-authorisation-data/ (archived at https://perma.cc/R7QF-XAY6)

7 Office for National Statistics. Consumer price inflation, UK, ONS, 2025. www.ons.gov.uk/economy/inflationandpriceindices/timeseries/czed/mm23 (archived at https://perma.cc/4D5X-9U5U)

8 Financial News. Impact of exchange rates on US–UK travel trends, Financial News, 2025. www.financial-news.co.uk/impact-of-exchange-rates-on-us-uk-travel-trends/ (archived at https://perma.cc/NH83-CVSS)

9 *Guardian*. Birth rate pushes UK population to greatest increase in almost 50 years, *Guardian*, 2009. www.theguardian.com/world/2009/aug/27/population-growth-uk-birth-rate-immigration (archived at https://perma.cc/U8GP-BDM3)

10 United States Census Bureau. Older people projected to outnumber children for first time in US History, United States Census Bureau, 2018. www.census.gov/newsroom/press-releases/2018/cb18-41-population-projections.html (archived at https://perma.cc/38S6-M5M9)

11 Office for National Statistics. Housing purchase affordability, UK: 2022, ONS, 2022. www.ons.gov.uk/peoplepopulationandcommunity/housing/bulletins/housingpurchaseaffordabilitygreatbritain/2022 (archived at https://perma.cc/9CT8-8RFB)

12 G Lee. Governments since 1997 have failed to build 600,000 houses, Channel 4, 2017. www.channel4.com/news/factcheck/governments-since-1997-have-failed-to-build-600000-houses (archived at https://perma.cc/3HJJ-2YW8)

13 Office for National Statistics. More adults living with their parents, ONS, 2023. www.ons.gov.uk/peoplepopulationandcommunity/populationandmigration/populationestimates/articles/moreadultslivingwiththeirparents/2023-05-10 (archived at https://perma.cc/S8BP-DL42)

14 McKinsey & Company. The state of tourism and hospitality 2024, McKinsey & Company, 2024. www.mckinsey.com/industries/travel/our-insights/the-state-of-tourism-and-hospitality-2024 (archived at https://perma.cc/DCC2-SWS4)

15 Kantar Media. Holiday trends 2025 report, Kantar Media, 2025. www.kantarmedia.com/reports/holiday-trends-2025-report (archived at https://perma.cc/3S9J-K3MP)

16 A Heathcote. Phocuswright Europe 2025, Adido Digital, 2025. www.adido-digital.co.uk/blog/phocuswright-europe-2025/ (archived at https://perma.cc/D8HJ-86PZ)

17 C Shu. Google acquires artificial intelligence startup DeepMind for more than $500m, Tech Crunch, 2014. techcrunch.com/2014/01/26/google-deepmind/ (archived at https://perma.cc/XDW5-YAPQ)

18 J Powell. Investors should not dismiss Cisco's dot-com collapse as a historical anomaly, FT, 2021. www.ft.com/content/81a03045-86f7-4e57-afbd-5ff83679615f (archived at https://perma.cc/E4DG-P22R)

19 R Fishkin. New research: Google Search grew 20 per cent+ in 2024; receives ~ 373X more searches than ChatGPT, Spark Toro, 2025. sparktoro.com/blog/new-research-google-search-grew-20-in-2024-receives-373x-more-searches-than-chatgpt/ (archived at https://perma.cc/UZ6J-H2AT)

20 A Santo. A complete (and actionable) Google update history timeline, Braton, 2025. www.brafton.co.uk/blog/seo/a-complete-and-actionable-google-update-history-timeline/ (archived at https://perma.cc/5YGW-NBGT)

21 R Fishkin. 2024 zero-click search study: For every 1,000 EU Google searches, only 374 clicks go to the open web. In the US, it's 360, Spark Toro, 2024. sparktoro.com/blog/2024-zero-click-search-study-for-every-1000-us-google-searches-only-374-clicks-go-to-the-open-web-in-the-eu-its-360/ (archived at https://perma.cc/8GAA-SUXV)

22 R Fishkin. Google CTR in 2018: Paid, organic, and no-click searches, Spark Toro, 2018. sparktoro.com/blog/google-ctr-in-2018-paid-organic-no-click-searches/ (archived at https://perma.cc/568H-TX2H)

23 P Mroke. Fake law leads, real money lost: How Google's AI ads are burning your budget—and how to stop it, ClearBox SEO, 2025. www.clearboxseo.com/how-googles-pmax-ads-are-burning-your-budget-and-how-to-stop-it/ (archived at https://perma.cc/CB5J-VZER)

24 *New York Post*. Mark Zuckerberg's Meta aims to fully automate advertising with AI by 2026: Report, *New York Post*, 2025. nypost.com/2025/06/02/business/meta-to-fully-automate-advertising-with-ai-by-2026-report/ (archived at https://perma.cc/JRP8-73SY)

25 The Verge. US vs Google: All the news from the search antitrust showdown, The Verge, 2025. www.theverge.com/23869483/us-v-google-search-antitrust-case-updates (archived at https://perma.cc/DP7P-48AN)

26 Corporate Europe Observatory. Lobbying power of Amazon, Google and Co. continues to grow, Corporate Europe Observatory, 2023. corporateeurope.org/en/2023/09/lobbying-power-amazon-google-and-co-continues-grow (archived at https://perma.cc/L69G-WXXR)

27 Skift. State of travel 2024, Skift, 2024. skift.com/insights/state-of-travel/ (archived at https://perma.cc/B3HU-VA9R)

INDEX

The main index is filed in alphabetical, word-by-word order. Acronyms and 'Mc' are filed as presented; numbers are filed as spelt out in full. Locators in italics denote information within a figure or table.

Looking for another book?

Explore our award-winning
books from global business
experts in Tourism, Leisure and
Hospitality

Scan the code to browse

www.koganpage.com/tlh

More from Kogan Page

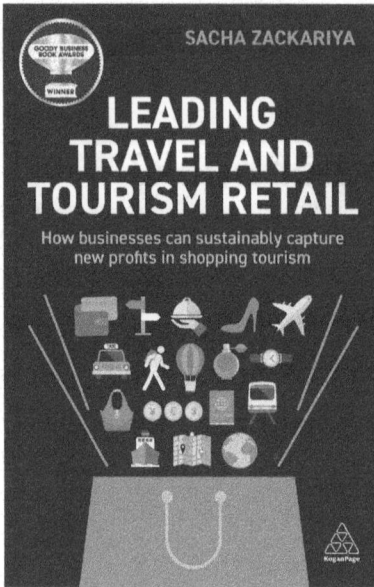

LEADING TRAVEL AND TOURISM RETAIL

SACHA ZACKARIYA

How businesses can sustainably capture new profits in shopping tourism

ISBN: 9781398609501

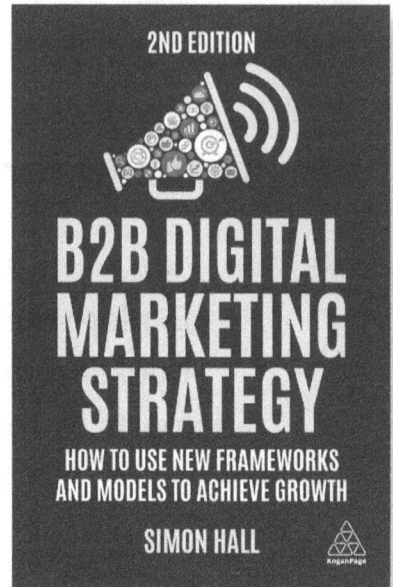

B2B DIGITAL MARKETING STRATEGY

2ND EDITION

HOW TO USE NEW FRAMEWORKS AND MODELS TO ACHIEVE GROWTH

SIMON HALL

ISBN: 9781398610170

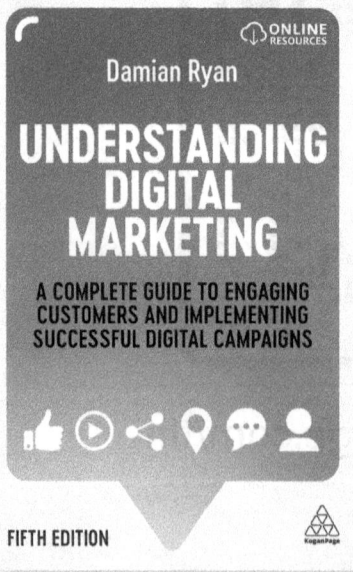

UNDERSTANDING DIGITAL MARKETING

Damian Ryan

A COMPLETE GUIDE TO ENGAGING CUSTOMERS AND IMPLEMENTING SUCCESSFUL DIGITAL CAMPAIGNS

FIFTH EDITION

ISBN: 9781789666014

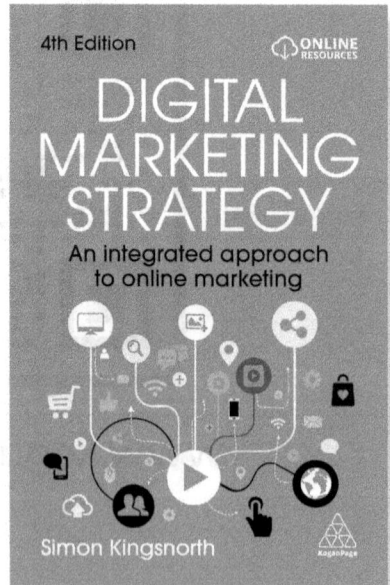

DIGITAL MARKETING STRATEGY

4th Edition

An integrated approach to online marketing

Simon Kingsnorth

ISBN: 9781398622067

www.koganpage.com

From 4 December 2025 the EU Responsible Person (GPSR) is:
eucomply oÜ, Pärnu mnt. 139b – 14, 11317 Tallinn, Estonia
www.eucompliancepartner.com

www.ingramcontent.com/pod-product-compliance
Lightning Source LLC
Chambersburg PA
CBHW071601210326
41597CB00019B/3353